T0131650

# THE 12

*Building Habits that Lead to
Spiritual Maturity*

ROGER NELMES

WESTBOW
PRESS®
A DIVISION OF THOMAS NELSON
& ZONDERVAN

This book is a work of non-fiction. Unless otherwise noted, the author
and the publisher make no explicit guarantees as to the accuracy of
the information contained in this book and in some cases, names of
people and places have been altered to protect their privacy.

WestBow Press books may be ordered through booksellers or by contacting:

WestBow Press
A Division of Thomas Nelson & Zondervan
1663 Liberty Drive
Bloomington, IN 47403
www.westbowpress.com
844-714-3454

Because of the dynamic nature of the Internet, any web addresses or
links contained in this book may have changed since publication and
may no longer be valid. The views expressed in this work are solely those
of the author and do not necessarily reflect the views of the publisher,
and the publisher hereby disclaims any responsibility for them.

Any people depicted in stock imagery provided by Getty Images are
models, and such images are being used for illustrative purposes only.
Certain stock imagery © Getty Images.

ISBN: 978-1-6642-9082-2 (sc)
ISBN: 978-1-6642-9083-9 (hc)
ISBN: 978-1-6642-9081-5 (e)

Library of Congress Control Number: 2023901675

Print information available on the last page.

WestBow Press rev. date: 04/19/2023

To my wife, Chrissy, and my three sons—Joshua, Jonathan, and Jordan—who have been on this journey with me from the beginning. To my parents, Steuart and Peggy, who have molded my Christian faith. Finally, to all the wonderful people who have allowed me the honor of leading them in small groups as they pursued a deeper relationship with Jesus.

# Praise For
## The 12

Are you searching for a resource to genuinely help you in your own spiritual maturity growth curve? Then SEARCH NO LONGER! "The 12" is the practical and game-changing resource you've been looking for. It was created and tested originally during the unforgettable COVID pandemic. But now, it has proven to be EXCEPTIONAL for Christians who want their level of discipleship to be stretched to a new and exciting level. It also includes a 12-week journal to help you chronicle your insights, growth, and personal reflections. Christian growth books are often "a dime a dozen." But this treasure by Roger Nelmes is one that could open a valuable path of growth for you personally. Disregard at your own peril.

***Dr. Jeanne Mayo***
Founder/Director THE CADRE
Founder/Director Youth Leader's Coach
Founder/Director PREVAIL Women's Mastermind Group
Author and popular public speaker

"So practical and enjoyable to read. Great teaching and breakdown of Scripture. I love how Roger gives useful next steps that can be used for the new or seasoned believer! Someone reading and finishing this book will gain tremendous hands-on teaching and application for growing in their walk with Jesus! I highly recommend giving this book out to people in your churches and small groups."

***Bradley Thomas***
Executive pastor of Immanuel Baptist Church

Show me your habits and I'll show you your future! This book will help you make and break the habits that will make or break you.

***Mark Batterson***
Pastor of National Community Church and New York Times best selling author

In an age where society is ever-attempting to set our habits, and draw our hearts towards things that will ultimately pass away, Roger builds a bold response to draw hearts back to what really matters. His passion and devotion to the way of Jesus is evident, as he explores what it means to be a disciple of Jesus through building habits that lead to spiritual maturity. –

**Daniel Groves**
Pastor of Hope City

# THIS BOOK BELONGS TO:

Name: _____

Phone Number: _____

Church: _____

Campus: _____

Start Date: _____

# CONTENTS

# INTRODUCTION

I can still remember my first roller-coaster ride. Angela Park, just outside my hometown of Hazleton, Pennsylvania, boasted a thirty-six-foot-tall wooden coaster built in 1957. The experience was less than enjoyable for me, but for the cute girl who convinced me to get on, it was a blast. My legs were wobbling as I attempted to get out of the car. My face was pale with one of those half-smile, half-deer-in-lights kind of expressions. Thankfully I didn't throw up, but I felt as if I had left part of me at the amusement park that day. It was years before I sat on another coaster, and yes, it was because a cute girl convinced me.

If you are anything like me, you've had moments in your journey of faith that seemed as if you were on a roller coaster. At times, it was only a little one, like that old wooden coaster at Angela Park. At times, it may have seemed like the SooperDooperLooper at Hershey Park, and it nearly sucked you right out of the safety harness. You experienced a significant spiritual awakening, where you felt the power and presence of God in deep, tangible ways; and then, like coming off a sugar rush, you crashed. You wondered, *How on earth did someone convince me to get on that thing?* Nonetheless, with the taste of vomit still in the back of your throat, you got right back in line for another ride.

Sometimes what transpired is obvious. Reality set in, and like Moses, you came down from Mount Sinai only to find the people in your life acting like fools. You threw down that experience like the Ten Commandments, shattering all God had done. At other times, you were hit with temptation as you came down from your spiritual high, and you stumbled into sin once again. Ashamed and embarrassed, you decided to linger there and wait for the next opportunity to get back on track. Little did you know that it would put you right back on the roller-coaster cycle once more.

I have seen this happen over and over again in youth ministry. Students show up to a youth service, respond to the love and mercy of God, and have an emotionally moving experience at the altar. Then a few days later, when the weekend begins, their spiritual awakening fades into the night. Weekend retreats and summer camps have a longer-lasting engagement, but for many, the end result is similar.

The spiritual roller coaster is all too real and acceptable in the modern church world. Its effect on our personal lives, not to mention the kingdom of God, is tremendously destabilizing. The roller-coaster life begins when we get comfortable ignoring the conviction of the Holy Spirit. Our comfort then leads to complacency. Complacency gives way to compromise. Compromise then fashions into carnality, a self-seeking and self-pleasuring lifestyle. This type of living isn't sustainable and cannot be acceptable.

A lack of conviction is what puts us on that roller coaster, and a lack of discipline is what keeps us there. Nobody wants to live like that. We all desire the stability and security of a consistent spiritual life. That's why you picked up this book in the first place.

The answer is never simple, and the road is never easy, but listen—that's a good thing. My youth pastor, Ken Clark, used to tell me something repeatedly. The message may have sunk in a little more each time I heard it, but it was still hard to hear. "Pain builds character," he said. Whether you are dealing with relational tension, trying to gain stamina while biking, or building a spiritual habit, the principle holds true. Your faith will be tested, but perseverance leads to maturity (James 1:2–8). Pain builds character.

I believe that through my pain, the testing of my faith, and especially my failures, perseverance lies within the complexity of disciplined habits. It is how I have been able to respond in faith as Paul did. "We are pressed on every side, but not crushed; perplexed, but not in despair; persecuted, but not abandoned; struck down, but not destroyed ... So then, death is at work in us, but life is at work in you" (2 Corinthians 4:8–12). This is how I am confident that "in all things God works for the good of those who love Him, who have been called according to His purpose" (Romans 8:28).

We are continually fighting a spiritual battle and therefore need to daily put on the armor of God (Ephesians 6:10–18). There is nothing casual or complacent about it. If you are tired of the roller-coaster life, you must live by the Spirit (Romans 8:1–17; Galatians 5:6.) That means daily building your faith by intentionally participating in spiritual disciplines.

Before you try to engage the tyranny of the urgent each morning, I challenge you to embrace the discomfort of building spiritual habits. Get up early if that's what it takes. Stay up late if you have to. Be disciplined and diligent, consistent, and concise. If it's easy, you're not doing it right. If it's not enjoyable and enlightening, you're definitely not doing it right.

My hope and prayer for you is that the five habits laid out in this book, with the additional template and prompts for practicing those habits, will help you. Before you turn to the next page, prepare your physical and spiritual space. Get your Bible, a highlighter, and an erasable pen or pencil. Then pause to pray. Invite the Holy Spirit to speak, move, and bring conviction and healing. He has been there the whole time, and He's ready to bring you wisdom and understanding.

## CHAPTER 1

# HIDE-AND-SEEK

Growing up as the youngest of twelve children had its challenges. To make matters worse, I was also the shortest, scrawniest kid in school. The only good thing about being tiny as a kid is when you're playing dodgeball or hide-and-seek. Luckily, I was great at both.

Actually, I was a master at hide-and-seek. I could get into the tiniest of places and never be found. My brothers and others gave up long before I revealed myself and risked giving up my perfect spots. Once I curled up in a pillowcase on the bed, and even with the lights on, they had no idea it was me.

I think people often view spiritual maturity a bit like playing hide-and-seek with God. At times we feel like the lights are out, and we are scurrying around, trying to find Him—trying to find the hidden or secret formula to being "spiritual." At other times, we hide because of doubt, failure, or sin—and we fall into the cycle where we feel that as we chase Him, He's hiding. And when He's chasing us, we're running away because we're afraid of being judged and punished.

In Matthew 6, Jesus is in the middle of the Sermon on the Mount and touching on a variety of subjects, such as generosity, prayer, fasting, storing up treasures in heaven, and worry. The common theme is that it all revolves around motives. Do you want to appear spiritual or truly draw near to God?

Spiritual maturity isn't a destination. Spiritual maturity isn't about how much you give but the fact that you give. It's not about how well you pray but that you pray. It's not about how much you fast but that you fast. Spiritual maturity is about the journey you take in getting to know God more. The key is found in verse 33. "But seek first His kingdom and His righteousness, and all these things will be given to you as well."

Spiritual maturity is about seeking *first* His kingdom and His righteousness. "First" speaks of priority and position. Until His kingdom does come, our spiritual formation continues to develop at the pace we are willing to follow.

To what lengths will you go to *seek* Him? Where does that seeking fall on your list of priorities? How are you actively chasing Jesus, after His kingdom and righteousness?

When COVID-19 first hit, I was in a nightmare of a slump. I had just spent six days in the hospital with meningitis, and I was in a state of depression—drained on every level. Then we went into lockdown, and our world was turned upside down. On top of that, my pastor resigned, I was miserable at work, and it was the one-year anniversary of my father's passing. I wasn't just locked down because of COVID. I felt locked down into this cycle of hide-and-seek with God. There I was, little Roger, looking for a pillowcase to hide in.

I knew I needed to *grow* through it and not just *go* through it. So I kept chasing Him, clinging to His faithfulness. As I read a devotional on the Bible app by Mark Batterson, I learned about the ministry of one of the greatest preachers, Charles Spurgeon. Even the "Prince of Preachers," as he was commonly referred to, faced struggles that brought him to a breaking point. He had great success; he pastored the largest church of his day, wrote 150 books, started a college, led over sixty charities, and was happily married with children, yet his life was marked by bouts of deep depression. Through all the success, stress, and struggles, he eventually came to the realization of his position in life. "I have learned to kiss the wave that throws me against the Rock of Ages"[1]

Reading those words was a moment of spiritual growth for me. So instead of hiding, I began embracing the wave. The Holy Spirit ministered to me and reminded me of what I'd already learned and experienced from Matthew 6:33.

1. Seeking His kingdom first is about making His purposes my priority. It is about "less of me and more of Him" (John 3:30). I needed to refocus, seek to serve others, and share my faith.
2. Seeking His righteousness first isn't just about not doing the things I know are bad, wrong, or against His will. It is about doing the right things He created me for so I can accomplish all He has called me to be.

Our church promotes a great next step for seekers and new believers called "The First 15." It's a challenge to spend five minutes every day in worship, five minutes reading the Bible, and five minutes praying. That doesn't sound like much, but in the days leading up to this, I was running on empty and struggled to meet this challenge. I'm sure you can relate.

On this day, however, I journaled something that caused a shift in the way I would "seek first." I felt a prompting to expand on that model and create what I called "The12." It's five simple spiritual habits practiced twelve minutes a day each, totaling sixty minutes (one hour). This was prompted by another profound statement of Jesus during the Sermon on the Mount from Matthew 5:6. "Blessed are those who hunger and thirst for righteousness, for they will be filled."

I've come to learn that the depth of my devotion is seen in my daily disciplines. My spiritual maturity depends on my willingness to seek Him first in everything. It's choosing consistency over complacency. It's submitting to conviction rather than compromise. It's about learning "to kiss the wave that throws me against the Rock of Ages."

Where do you see yourself regarding your spiritual maturity? Go ahead and give yourself a score between 1 and 10, with 1 being the lowest and 10 being the highest. _____ At what point on that scale would you consider someone hiding and another seeking?

_____

_____

_____

_____

_____

_____

_____

_____

_____

Let me ask you again. To what lengths will you go to *seek* Him? Be brave and write it down.

_____

_____

_____

_____

_____

_____

_____

_____

_____

## CHAPTER 2

# ARE YOU HUNGRY?

When I was about ten years old, my brothers, Doug and Brian, and one of the neighborhood boys were playing in some fresh snow. We loved the snow. We built forts, had great snowball fights, and played king of the hill. The winner of these epic skirmishes got to keep the fort.

I don't remember who was on my team that day, but I know my team won. We were celebrating in my fort when one of my older brothers decided to take revenge and jump on our roof, caving it in on top of us. I could barely move and was convinced I would suffocate.

I doubt my life was ever truly in jeopardy, but as a kid, I did what kids do. I freaked out. I screamed and perhaps cried a bit, but we won't talk about that. When I finally dug my way out, I yelled at my brother and even dropped an f-bomb. It may have been the first time I ever said that word (and unfortunately, not the last).

I watched as my brother's face quickly changed from slight fear that I might have been injured to blissful glee that he had witnessed something to hold over my head. This was sibling rivalry at its worst. Our battle for king of the hill wasn't over.

"Oh, I'm telling Mom and Dad!" he said with a contentious smile. Not that I was the little angel of the family, but I was the youngest and simply hadn't had as many opportunities to mess up yet. Nevertheless, this was a big mess-up, and I was scared of the consequences.

My parents were pretty strict, and I knew a good spanking was in my near future. More than the punishment, the look of disappointment on my mom's face would be more than I could bear. So, to avoid that outcome, I decided to run away. That would solve everything.

I started walking down the street, headed to who knows where, my brother's voice getting farther and farther out of range. Maybe after I couldn't hear him anymore, the guilty feeling would go away. I was testing the theory of "out of sight, out of mind." As long as I didn't see my parents again, I wouldn't have to face the punishment.

Then I realized that the sound of his voice was replaced by the sound of footsteps running toward me. I turned around and saw that it was my other older brother, Doug, and he asked what I was doing. "I'm running away," I told him. So, he did as big brothers do: he joined me and convinced his friend to do so as well.

A few miles into our walk, it was getting dark, and we were exhausted. We sat on the side of a hill in the woods, just off the main road. Reality started to set in, and we contemplated whether running away was really the best idea. After all, it was the middle of winter, we'd already spent our three dollars and change, and like I said, it was getting dark. So we admitted defeat and headed back home.

I remember sneaking into the back door of our house and just standing there. It was so warm in the house compared to outside, but I was still shaking in my boots while thinking about how mad my parents must be. Just then, my mom walked in and saw me. I was caught.

I'm not sure if she even realized I had run away at that point. I wasn't sure whether my other brother had shared about my potty mouth either. To be honest, I can't remember any of those details.

But what I do remember more than anything was that rather than a spanking, she sent me to bed without dinner. Tragically, it was pizza night. Not just homemade or frozen pizza either. It was delivery! That rarely happened at the Nelmes's home.

That night I went to bed with an empty stomach and a lot of regrets. I was grateful to be warm and in my own bed rather than under the stars, but it was difficult to fall asleep. I could hear my guilty conscience almost as loud as my stomach growling in hunger. If not for sheer exhaustion, I probably wouldn't have slept at all.

When I woke up the next morning, I was starving. After all, I was a growing boy. It was Saturday, and that usually meant a big, hot breakfast like scrambled eggs, pancakes, or French toast. I anxiously walked down the stairs, unsure of what to expect. Would my parents still be mad? What punishment still awaited me? Would I be permitted to eat now?

Well, I've obviously lived to tell the story. Yes, I got the third degree and was grounded for what seemed like an eternity. I had some explaining and apologizing to do. The experience was humbling but necessary. However, those pancakes that morning never tasted so good!

This story carries lessons on different levels, but let me share how I see it fitting with a very famous verse from Matthew 5:6. This will help set the foundation for this journal. "Blessed are those who hunger and thirst for righteousness, for they will be filled."

First, I think far too often, people choose to run away because they feel their mess-ups are too messy for God to handle. Have you ever thought about that? Maybe you have had some negative experiences with how people have handled your failures. Perhaps you are your worst critic, and you have condemned yourself to the point that guilt keeps you from looking in the mirror.

If that's you, allow me to remind you of what Jesus said after being falsely accused, brutally beaten, spat on, publicly ridiculed, and hung on the cross to die. He said, "Father, forgive them, for they know not what they do" (Luke 23:34). He is a forgiving God.

Listen to the words of David in Psalm 136, where in all twenty-six verses he repeats, "His love endures forever." Remember, David slept with another man's wife and sent her husband to the front line to be killed in battle, yet David experienced God's enduring love and grace when he repented.

Your mistakes, no matter how many or messy, aren't too much for His love. Will there be consequences? Unfortunately, yes. Will it be difficult at times? Of course. Will His love ever change? Never! Read that again. His love for you will never change.

A second point is that we need to get hungry and thirsty for the right stuff. After missing dinner that night, I was so hungry the next morning that I probably would have eaten just about anything. My mom's pancakes for breakfast didn't just fill my belly—they satisfied my needs on many levels.

When Jesus said, "Blessed are those who hunger and thirst for righteousness, for they will be filled," He used terminologies that originally applied to the feeding and fattening of animals. Animals will overeat if you let them. If you've ever had a pet, you know it's true. When I feed my dog, he chomps it down like he hasn't been fed in days. Then I'll walk away, and he will act like he's still hungry. My wife will see that look in his eyes, and, not knowing I just fed him, she will feed him again. He will eat until he makes himself sick.

We can fill our lives with so many things, but do they really satisfy our longings? Jesus told us that He came to give us life to the fullest. The Amplified Version says, "I came that they may have life and have it in abundance [to the full, till it overflows]" (John 10:10).

If we hunger and thirst for the right stuff—His righteousness—He will fill us. He will fatten us up. He will give us more than we deserve—to the full, till it overflows. That is what this journey is all about. When we realize and accept His forgiveness of all our past failures and sins, and then hunger for *His* right stuff, we will be greater blessed than I was that morning while eating my mom's pancakes. Are you hungry?

CHAPTER 3

# THE12

In 1969, the Children's Television Workshop created *Sesame Street*, what would quickly become an American Institution and cultural phenomenon. Funded by government and private foundations, the children's program used Jim Henson's Muppets and included short films with humor and cultural references. Their goal was to create a children's television show that would "master the addictive qualities of television and do something good with them,"[1] such as helping young children prepare for school.

One such iconic short film from *Sesame Street* that stuck with me was the 1977 "Pinball Number Count" sung by the Pointer Sisters. It was insanely catchy and took place in an animated fantasy pinball machine every kid would love to play (well, maybe back in the day). If you have ever seen it, I am confident that it's stuck in your head now.

"One-two-three
four-five
six-seven-eight nine-ten
eleven-twelve!"[2]

As believers, when we hear someone talk about "the Twelve," we typically think about the twelve disciples who traveled with Jesus for over three years until His death and resurrection. Those twelve men then spearheaded the formation of the early church and evangelization of the known world.

My idea of The12 is not a catchy children's song, although I want it to be as repetitive and memorable. Nor is this book about the disciples, although I want it to be as impactful. The concept of The12 is simply developing five key spiritual habits by practicing them for twelve minutes a day with the encouragement and accountability of friends. The five habits are worship, devotion, journaling, prayer, and encouraging others. Spending twelve minutes a day on each habit will cost you only one hour a day. The return on investment is guaranteed to be exponentially greater. Building these habits in your daily life will lead you to a place of spiritual maturity.

I have been in ministry for over twenty-five years. What I have discovered is that regardless of age, gender, race, or economic status, the underlying cause for struggle in the believer's life is the lack of spiritual discipline. We usually know enough to attend church, but we lack the spiritual fortitude to walk out our faith. The hardest part of that reality is the truth that not only does that hold us back from experiencing the full life God has created us for, but it also means our potential for building the kingdom of God and influencing the world for Christ is wasted.

We need to realize that at salvation, we started a new life. "The old has passed away; behold, the new has come" (2 Corinthians 5:17). Now we should "like newborn babies, crave pure spiritual milk, so that by it you may grow up in your salvation, now that you have tasted that the Lord is good" (1 Peter 2:2–3). Why is this so important? Because "you are a chosen people, a royal priesthood, a holy nation, God's special possession, *that you may declare the praises of him who called you* out of darkness into his wonderful light" (1 Peter 2:9, emphasis added). There is more to life than just surviving. There is more to life than just attending church. Jesus wants an everyday, ongoing relationship with you. He wants for you more than you can imagine.

In the pages that follow, you will find twelve weeks' worth of prompts to help you begin and develop your habits. Each week begins with a short summary of various biblical principles. Then pages provided for Monday through Saturday include suggested scripture readings, worship songs, and space for journaling and recording your prayers. For Sunday there are pages for weekly reflections and space to take notes while attending your church worship service.

As with anything, starting is always the hardest part. What are some things you will need to say *no* to so you can say *yes* to the time and energy required to establish these habits? When is the best time of day that will allow you to make the most of your efforts? Where is a good place for you to be alone and away from distractions?

Probably the most important question that remains is, who can join you on this journey? I am a firm believer that we aren't meant to do life alone. Whom can you ask to hold you accountable and help keep you on track? Can they also participate in The12 with you as a small group? Jot a few names down. Pray over them. Then swallow your pride and ask those people to walk alongside you in the process. You won't regret it! "I am certain that *God*, who began a good work within you, will continue *His* work until it is finally *finished*" (Philippians 1:6 NLT, emphasis added).

## Worship

Jesus always seems to go out of His way to be in the right place at the wrong time, like when He arrived at Bethany four days after Lazarus had died (John 11:1–44). Sometimes He showed up at the wrong place but at the right time. Consider Jesus when He went to the Sheep Gate to heal the man who had been an invalid for thirty years. He didn't go to fancy places to minister to the rich and elite. He went to where the dregs of society lived under the bridge (John

5:1–14). At another time He even entered the scene at the wrong place and wrong time as He walked on water three to three and a half miles in the middle of the night while a terrible storm was brewing (John 6:19–21).

Jesus was very intentional in everything He did, regardless of the time or place. The story of the woman at the well is another perfect example. In John 4, Jesus went out of His way to be in the right place at the right time, no matter how wrong it appeared. Jewish people didn't typically travel through Samaria. In fact, they usually went out of their way to go around it. A rabbi wouldn't stop to have a conversation with a Samaritan woman—especially an adulterous one her own people were ashamed of. Yet amid racial, religious, and political prejudices, Jesus used this opportunity to speak to a nonbelieving outcast about the heart of worship.

After defining the place of worship and the order of worship as secondary to our spiritual relationship with God, Jesus described real worship. According to Him, worship would take on two new aspects: it would be in spirit and in truth. If we are not worshipping "in spirit," our worship will be dry and lifeless. Worship not done "in truth" becomes deceitful or irrelevant. "In spirit" reminds us of who we are worshipping.[3]

In this divine appointment moment, Jesus used the basic need of thirst to reveal spiritual truth. Worship is no longer about a place but about a position. It's no longer about a building but a bonding. Worship is in spirit because it is when our inner person—that God-breathed part of us that responded to grace in faith—connects with God, who is spirit. It isn't an event but a response to a relationship.

At the heart of worship is Jesus. At the heart of Jesus is the forgiveness of sin: salvation. When we acknowledge who Jesus is as the Son of God and the Savior of mankind, we begin to worship in spirit and truth. Worship is no longer about ritualistic obligation but about reverent obedience. Worship isn't about style but substance. Worship is the expression of genuine obedience. It's not an event but an action.

One of the Old Testament words for "worship" is *shachah*—to kneel, stoop, prostrate oneself, or throw oneself down in reverence. The New Testament word for "worship" is *proskuneo*. This Greek term literally means kissing, bowing down, and showing respect and adoration.[4]

Our modernized idea of worship is typically limited to music. However, we see from both the Old and New Testament definitions that worship can be anything that demonstrates worth and adoration to God. It can be anything that connects our affection to the heart of God and brings Him glory. Worship can include meditating on His Word, loving our neighbor, serving our community, demonstrating generosity to someone in need, tithing, praying, playing an instrument, painting, writing, dancing, singing, clapping, raising our hands in surrender, kneeling down—and the list goes on.

Even with this realization of all the various ways we can worship, the unfortunate reality is that many believers tend to limit their expressions of worship to a weekend corporate experience. That weekend mentality weakens our original intent. We were created for worship, and our ultimate purpose is to bring honor and glory to our creator, God. We shouldn't confine our purpose to a one-hour "worship experience" in a church service.

Jesus also told us that our purpose is to let our light shine so that the world will see how good God is and glorify Him (Matthew 5:16). If the only day we turn on our light is Sunday and that occurrence is mostly with other "lights" or believers, how then will the world have an opportunity to see it?

What if Daniel hadn't prayed facing out his window three times a day? What if the Israelites hadn't marched around the walls of Jericho? What if Paul and Silas hadn't prayed and sung while in prison? Our worship in its various forms is an expression of love and devotion to God. But it is also a means of demonstrating the glory of God—putting Him on center stage.

Yes, corporate times of worshipping as a church are important. Private times of worship need to be a daily spiritual discipline as well. This will develop a lifestyle of worship that is expressed in everything we do. Spirit and truth worship moments should be expressed in such a way that causes the world to stand up and notice the glory of God. "Therefore, I urge you, brothers and sisters, in view of God's mercy, to offer your bodies as a living sacrifice, holy and pleasing to God—this is your true and proper worship" (Romans 12:1).

His sacrifice for our sins is now our sacred calling to worship. Every day is a worship experience, where we put our lives on display for His glory (see Hebrews 9:14).

Worship Challenge

Understanding that public worship should be preceded by private worship, accept this challenge to include the habit of worship as a catalyst for next-level lifestyle worship.

1. Find a time and place free of distraction where you can have intentional time with God for worship using music for twelve minutes.
2. Create a song list of your own or use the suggested songs provided in the journal portion of this book. The challenge is to listen and understand the words you're singing. I personally like to use YouTube, since it often has the lyrics included and makes me feel as if I am there in the moment.
3. As you sing, visualize the words and your expressions to God. Make the song or songs relevant to you.
4. Be open and invite the Holy Spirit to join you.
5. Be expressive.

**Prayer**

Prayer shouldn't scare or intimidate us. Prayer is simply an opportunity to personally connect to God through direct communication. It's a simple conversation with God. This conversation, however, is a two-way street of not just talking but also listening. Prayer is our lifeline, which draws us into intimacy with God while teaching us to hear His voice. It is how we actively let God know the desires of our hearts, our needs, and our wants.

Prayer is an absolutely essential tool for the believer's life. James tells us, "The prayer of a righteous person is powerful and effective" (James 5:16). Without prayer in our lives, it can feel like we are trying to chop down a sequoia tree with a pocketknife. But in prayer we have access to the throne room of God, where He hears the prayers of His people.

The disciples of Jesus knew how to pray, yet they saw an obvious difference between their prayers and the ones Jesus prayed. When Jesus prayed, water turned to wine, a few fish and loaves of bread fed thousands, the sick were healed, the blind received their sight, and the dead were raised.

I think it's interesting that of all the things the disciples could have asked Jesus to teach them to be able to do, they chose prayer. Why not ask Him how to preach or to be bold enough to stand against the Pharisees? Why not ask Him how to turn water into wine or to speak in parables? Instead: "When he had finished [praying], one of his disciples said to him, 'Lord, teach us to pray, just as John taught his disciples'" (Luke 11:1).

After Jesus gave His disciples some logistics about prayer, Matthew's version of the Lord's Prayer begins, "This, then, is how you should pray" (Matthew 6:9). Jesus then proceeded to give them a prayer pattern to follow. This isn't just a prayer to be recited but a pattern to be followed (read Matthew 6:9–13).

"Our Father in heaven, hallowed be your name."

Here we see our need to come to God as a child approaches his or her loving father. It also reminds us that He is in heaven, watching and caring over every aspect of our lives. He is, however, also holy and worthy of our worship, so we need to approach prayer with a thankful heart. How can you honor God in your time spent in prayer? What are some things you can thank Him for?

_____

_____

_____

"Your kingdom come, your will be done, on earth as it is in heaven."

You often hear pastors pray these words over their church. This shows us that before we come to him with a list of what we want, we pray for His desires and plans over our lives and the world around us. Are there ways in which you aren't seeking God's kingdom over your own life? How does Matthew 6:33 help to explain how we are to pray?

"Give us this day our daily bread."

After honoring Him and surrendering to His plans, now we pray over our basic needs and the needs of those around us. Make a list of a few things you are praying over your own life and a few you are praying for concerning your friends or family.

| You | Others |
|-----|--------|
| _____ | _____ |
| _____ | _____ |
| _____ | _____ |

"And forgive us our debts, as we also have forgiven our debtors."

Here we can see the necessity not only to acknowledge our mistakes and ask for forgiveness but also to extend mercy and grace to others by forgiving them. What are some things you need to ask forgiveness for? Is there someone to whom you need to express your forgiveness (see also vv. 14–15)?

_____

_____

_____

"And lead us not into temptation, but deliver us from the evil one."

Pray for the Spirit to reveal your weakness and for the power to overcome temptation. Ask for wisdom to set up boundaries to avoid areas of temptation. What are some things for which you need to ask God to give you strength to overcome or avoid in your life?

_____

_____

_____

Over the next few weeks, use this as your prayer pattern. I also suggest that you find a place alone and away from distractions so you can focus your attention on God and the conversation you are trying to have with him (see Luke 5:16). It might also be helpful to use the same time every day and make it a habit. Consistency is always key in creating a lasting and productive habit.

What do Proverbs 15:8, 29; and Psalm 145:18–19 say about how God listens to us?

_____

_____

_____

Where and when will you spend your time in prayer?

_____

What can you do to help your prayer time be consistent and free from distractions?

_____

_____

_____

_____

## Devotion: Meditating on Scripture

Growing up in northeast Pennsylvania afforded us the privilege of experiencing all four seasons, each of which had its own appeal. To me, though, fall was especially beautiful. It was sweater weather, leaves were changing, and the smell of football season was in the air.

Almost every weekend in the fall, the neighborhood kids met up at the elementary school to play football. Being the smallest kid on the field was a bit intimidating when it came to trying to tackle someone, but when I had the ball, I had some advantages. Quick and slippery, I could duck under most of their attempts to grab me. It was so much fun.

Once, however, a young man on the opposing team didn't like my elusiveness. He decided enough was enough. The next time I ran by him, he decided to kick my feet out from under me. When he did, I spun around in a 360 and went vertical, with my arms outstretched like Superman, my belly flopping right on top of the football. The fall knocked the wind right out of me. I gasped for air over and over, but I just couldn't breathe.

I eventually caught my breath, but it wasn't a good experience. I didn't really think I would die, but the reality is, if you can't breathe, you can't live. Breathing is conducive to life.

In the story of creation, we see that God formed man out of the dust of the earth on the sixth day. As if that wasn't extraordinary enough, He did something in creating Adam that was unique to all His other creations. "He breathed the breath of life into the man's nostrils, and the man became a living person" (Genesis 1:27). Man wasn't living until he had the breath of God in him. That is physical life.

However, the next chapter reveals how sin entered the world and brought with it God's wrath and ultimately, death. Physical death is inevitable. "Therefore, just as sin entered the world through one man, and death through sin, and in this way, death came to all people, because all sinned" (Romans 5:12).

Thankfully, that isn't where the story ends. Continue reading, and you will find Paul describing the gift of grace. Just as one man's sin brought condemnation on humanity, one man's sacrifice brought justification—the removal of all guilt. As one of my Bible school professors put it, His grace makes it just as if I've never sinned. I simply need to confess with my mouth that Jesus is Lord and believe in my heart that God raised him from the dead, and I will be saved (see Romans 10:9). This is spiritual life.

As if that wasn't enough of a blessing—physical life and spiritual life—His grace extends even further with the gift of His Holy Spirit. As he foretold His coming death to His disciples, He promised to send "another," an advocate—the Paraclete (*parakletos* in John 14:16) or Holy Spirit—to come alongside those who believe to teach, guide, intercede, comfort, support, help, and be our friend.[5]

Then in John 20, appearing to the disciples as they hid behind locked doors, Jesus "breathed on them and said, 'Receive the Holy Spirit.'" Not long after, on the day of Pentecost, about 120 believers were filled with the Holy Spirit and launched a revival that birthed the Christian church. This is the Spirit-filled life.

To summarize, God's breath gave man physical life at creation. Jesus gave up His breath to give man spiritual life through salvation. The Holy Spirit, then, was first received through the resurrected Christ breathing on the disciples and then to the 120 as wind blew through the upper room.

All this information and inspiration is made possible through the written word of scripture. "All scripture is God-breathed and is useful for teaching, rebuking, correcting and training in righteousness, so that the servant of God may be thoroughly equipped for every good work" (2 Timothy 3:16–17).

The Bible—scripture—is "God-breathed," meaning it is inspired by God. It is the supernatural influence of the Holy Spirit on the writers of scripture. God used men—their style and personality—but empowered and anointed them to pen His word, which substantiates its accuracy and trustworthiness. Warren Wiersbe wrote, "Revelation means the communicating of truth to man by God; inspiration has to do with the recording of the communication in a way that is dependable."[6]

Paul informed Timothy not only of the inspiration of scripture but also of its benefits. "And [it] is useful for teaching, rebuking, correction in training in righteousness."

The Greek word for "teaching" is *didaskalia*. It means to provide instruction, teaching material; the practice of instructing another in an area of knowledge.[7] It involves the process of learning.

When reading and studying scripture, we ask the following:

1. What does this passage tell me about who God is?
2. What has God done, or what is He still doing?
3. In light of what has been discovered, what should I now do?

"Rebuking" is defined as convincing by means of proof that someone has done something wrong. It is the Greek word *elegmos*. Trench, a biblical scholar, defines *rebuking* as to "rebuke another with such a factual wielding of the virtuous arm of truth, as to bring him, if not always to a confession, yet at least to a conviction of his sin."[8] This brings the opportunity of repentance.

1. Is an area of fault being exposed?
2. What beliefs are my behavior revealing?
3. Where do I need to admit I was wrong or sinful?

"Correction," *epanorthosis* in the Greek, is the "restoration to an upright or right state, to make correct or improve."[9] This brings us to a greater or more firm belief. Here we ask the following:

1. What didn't I know, and how does that now change my belief or behavior?
2. Where do I need to make a course correction?

"Training in righteousness," the Greek word *paideia*, refers to the whole training and education process, which relates to the cultivation of mind and morals, showing people how to please and glorify God.[10] "Righteousness" basically means right living. It is living the life God created for us and freed us to live in. This is the process of obedience and application of truth. Here is where we ask the following:

1. In what areas do I need to trust and obey?
2. How can I please and glorify God with what I am learning?

For me, the best part of this verse is the final phrase; it is the "so that" statement. "So that the man of God may be adequate, equipped for every good work" (v. 17 NASB).

"Thoroughly," or adequate as the New American Standard Bible translates it, means to be "acceptable, qualified, or proficient."[11] To be "equipped" carries the idea of being fitted for the task. The Word of God equips God's people to do God's work. The better we know His Word, the better we can live for Him and accomplish what He has created us for.

In the journaling pages to come, there are suggested Bible reading prompts for you. As you read them, give yourself permission to underline key words or phrases. Jot down questions and take note of any "aha" moments. Use the journal to record your thoughts and track what you read and learned, and how you can apply it (see the example in the journal section*).

## Why Journal?

A journal is basically a record of your day-by-day activities, which you feel are meaningful enough to remember by jotting them down. Some people use a journal more as a diary of their intimate thoughts and feelings. Others use a journal as part of an experiential learning process to reflect and grow.

Use this journal as a tool for creating routines and tracking your spiritual growth. Feel free to mix it up as you feel comfortable, but we have provided some specific markers for you as a road map for your journey.

Each daily page asks you what you are reading, what you are learning, and how you are applying it to your daily life. These questions are simply a guide to assist you while creating patterns for growth as you connect to God. Write down the Bible portion you read and what really spoke to you; then describe how what you just learned will help shape your behavior and faith.

We have also provided a Weekly Reflection for you to summarize your experiences and take a look at the bigger picture of how you are connecting to God. Here you can also reflect on the changes you are growing through in your personal discipleship process. There is also additional space provided for you to take notes on the weekend message, books you are reading, or ideas for implementing through active ministry.

*Take a look at the sample page for more details about how you can use this journal.

Example

**What Did You Read?**
Ephesians 2

**What Did You Learn?**
Verse 10 was very pivotal for me. "We are His workmanship"—His masterpiece, one of a kind. We are much more valuable to God than we realize, even more so than the *Mona Lisa*. But He didn't make us just to hang us on a wall. He created us to "do good works."

**How Can You Apply What You Have Learned to Your Daily Life?**

Since I now realize I am saved by grace through my faith in Jesus and because I know I am a masterpiece made for the purpose of good works, I need to stop trying to earn His attention and start doing because I love Him and want to bring Him honor and glory.

Work toward unity. It doesn't matter what our pasts were like or what our religious backgrounds are. Our nationality, economic status, and skin color are of no consequence. God obviously wants us to work together for the common good of building His church.

**Prayer**

Help me to see myself as You see me—a one-of-a-kind masterpiece.

Help me to step out in faith to "do good works" for Your glory.

Help me to be accepting and loving toward others.

## Encouraging Others

One of my favorite Bible verses is Hebrews 10:24. For me it speaks to the necessity of activity for everyday life as a believer. We see it lived out as Jesus traveled with the disciples. We also see this as the foundation of the formation of the early church in Acts. It is living life together with the intentional mindset of influencing those around us to know God and make Him known. "And let us consider how we may spur one another on toward love and good deeds, not giving up meeting together, as some are in the habit of doing, but encouraging one another—and all the more as you see the Day approaching" (Hebrews 10:24–25).

There is a statement we use at our church all the time. "What fills, spills." In other words, whatever I fill my life with—what I watch or listen to, what goes into my head and heart—is going to spill out in what I say, how I say it, what I do, and how I do it. (Read Galatians 6:8; Romans 6:13 for more.) If we are truly filling our lives with His Word, worship, and prayer, then the natural by-product should be for those things to then spill over into our daily lives.

Paul encourages the church, "Let the message about Christ, in all its richness, fill your lives. Teach and counsel each other with all the wisdom he gives. Sing psalms and hymns and spiritual songs to God with thankful hearts" (Colossians 3:16 NLT). The word *teach* means to "impart knowledge in a formal or informal setting." And to "counsel" means to "admonish or advise someone concerning dangerous consequences, to warn or even to reprimand firmly."

I believe these scriptures are telling us that the presence of God should be so overwhelming in our lives that we are continually encouraging others by sharing what we are learning (teach), challenging their lifestyle (counsel), and stirring their faith to action (spur toward love and good deeds).

So what would that look like for you? How can you make time to encourage others daily as part of your spiritual disciplines? Those are questions only you can answer, but here are a few suggestions.

1. Make it a matter of prayer. As you spend daily time in the other disciplines of Bible reading, journaling, worshipping, and praying, ask God for wisdom, creativity, and discernment to know what to share and whom to share it with.
2. Look for opportunities and make the most of them. Every conversation we have is an opportunity to encourage someone. Look for the opening to share what God is doing in your life. (Read Ephesians 5:16; Colossians 4:5.)
3. Be ready to share your story. Jesus said we are the light of the world, a city on a hill that can't be hidden (Matthew 5:14). People will notice the difference in your life as you get closer to Jesus. You will become a reflection of His glory! Be ready to give a reason for the hope that is in you (1 Peter 3:15). I would encourage you to have a thirty- to sixty-second version and a three- to five-minute version of your story ready to share.

## CHAPTER 4

# YOUR JOURNEY BEGINS HERE

I can still remember quite vividly when I started dating my wife, Chrissy, in college. With her being six foot tall and me being only five seven, I was amazed she even noticed me, let alone wanted to date me. Well, to be honest, I had to do some convincing.

When I think about it, I recall that I worked pretty hard to get noticed. I did some investigating to find out what her class schedule was, and then I made a point to position myself where she walked by. I did reconnaissance to watch what she ate, learn who her friends were, and discover what intrigued her. Then I looked for moments to engage in conversation with the things I had learned about her. Sounds a bit like stalking, doesn't it? I wasn't creepy about it—I promise. Well, maybe you should ask her, just to be sure.

When we started dating, I did what everyone does in an attempt to capture someone's attention and win his or her heart. I showered, lathered myself in Obsession cologne, slicked my hair back, and put on my snakeskin boots to give me an extra inch and a half of height. I wrote her poems and songs. I sweet-talked her and told her how amazing she was. I bought her a hot cup of tea, sat across the table from her, stared deeply into her eyes, listened intently to everything she said, and placed my foot right against hers in hopes to have hers brush up against mine. I know, I know. It sounds a little pathetic. Yet it still gives me goose bumps just thinking about it.

The truth is, I wasn't playing. I had made some serious mistakes in previous relationships. Perhaps you've been there. Before I started chasing after my wife, I had searched for relational fulfillment. I desperately wanted to be loved, desired, admired, given attention to, and be the center of someone else's world. I even thought I had it once, until someone else showed me more of what I thought I wanted. After disappointment, heartache, and a touch of reality, I walked away, expecting that what I wanted either wasn't possible or just wasn't meant for me. As so many are good at doing, I gave up.

When Chrissy walked into that college student union and I saw her for the first time, big hair and all bundled up from the snowy January weather, something stirred in me. No, it wasn't just my hormones. It was hope. It was an awakening of sorts. There was a shift in every part of my being. A belief in new possibilities.

I asked the young man sitting next to me, "Who is that girl?"

With a smirk, he said, "That's my sister," and he stood to give her a big hug. He must have seen my glossed-over eyes as I watched her walk into the room. I imagine everyone saw my reaction. It was difficult to hide, but I really didn't care.

These are some amazing memories for me. I can talk about them for hours. Thirty years later, I still get emotional while reminiscing about the journey. Every page of our story, the good and the not so good, speaks not only of where we've been but also of where we are going. There are many lessons we've learned and others we are still learning. One day at a time.

I think Ziad Abdelnour said it perfectly: "Life is like a camera. Focus on what is important. Capture the good times. Develop from the negatives. And if things don't work out, take another shot."[1]

I'm so grateful for my wife and even more so for my relationship with my first love, Jesus. I remember how He pursued me and positioned Himself in the middle of every chapter of my story. Without fail, every time I responded to the intersection of His story with mine, history was made.

You are on a journey of your own—most importantly, a pursuit of love with your Father God. The beautiful truth of our pursuit of God is that He is pursuing us even more. He's not turned off by our faults and failures. He's not mad at our many mistakes. He wants and desires a relationship with us.

As a young man, I was taught that in a relationship, love is spelled t-i-m-e. We choose how to spend our time, and it demonstrates our capacity to love and be loved. Time spent with those we love is our effort in preparing for more—greater, deeper, longer, and more intimate love.

Albert Einstein is credited for saying, "The best preparation for the future is to live as if there were none." I think we would all agree that we need to make the most of every relationship, especially the one we have with God.

The next section of this book is the journal of your journey with Jesus. It's your opportunity to make the most of your love—your time, your pursuit of growing with God. It's set up to help you walk through what I've called "The12," that is, twelve minutes in five spiritual disciplines: worship, prayer, devotion, journaling, and encouraging others.

It is worth repeating that you should find a quiet place and intentional time for these disciplines. Use the suggested worship songs and scripture portions or find your own. The program will probably be a little uncomfortable. It's going to be a sacrifice. However, here's what I know: you will get more out of it than what you put into it. Get into a rhythm and be consistent.

"How is that?" you may ask. Because God's economy is nothing like ours. He is in the habit of taking little and multiplying it. He is looking for the opportunity to take our few fish and loaves of bread and feed the thousands with plenty left over. He wants to take your willingness to grow in these simple steps and build you into the man or woman of God He has created and called you to become.

Hopefully, you're not afraid of a challenge, progress, commitment, or a blank page. If you are, well, this is where all that needs to change. Paul encourages his readers not to be anxious about anything, but rather, in every situation we are to pray, be thankful, and ask Him for peace and clarity (see Philippians 4:6–7).

You don't need to be intimidated by the blank pages ahead. There is no reason to worry about how your prayers may sound. Your level of biblical literacy isn't in question. Simon Cowell isn't there to judge your vocal agility as you worship. This is about seeking Him. It's about our hunger and thirst. Here is where you decide how hungry you are. Here is where you will be blessed and filled.

Are you ready? Then let's begin.

# Songs for Worship

1. "It Is Well" by Bethel Music
2. "Surrounded" by Upper Room

**What Did You Read?**
Matthew 5:1–64, Sermon on the Mount, Part 1

**What Did You Learn?**

_____

_____

_____

_____

_____

_____

**How Can You Apply What You Have Learned to Your Daily Life?**

_____

_____

_____

_____

_____

_____

**Prayer**

_____

_____

_____

_____

_____

## Songs for Worship

1. "Set a Fire" by Jesus Culture, Chris Quilala
2. "O Come to the Altar" by Elevation Worship

**What Did You Read?**
Matthew 6:4–7:29, Sermon on the Mount, Part 2

**What Did You Learn?**

_____

_____

_____

_____

_____

**How Can You Apply What You Have Learned to Your Daily Life?**

_____

_____

_____

_____

_____

**Prayer**

_____

_____

_____

_____

_____

## Songs for Worship

1. "Great Are You Lord" by All Sons & Daughters
2. "Way Maker" by Leeland

**What Did You Read?**
Matthew 13:1–58, The Kingdom of Heaven

**What Did You Learn?**

_____
_____
_____
_____
_____
_____

**How Can You Apply What You Have Learned to Your Daily Life?**

_____
_____
_____
_____
_____
_____

**Prayer**

_____
_____
_____
_____
_____
_____

## *Songs for Worship*

1. "How He Loves" by David Crowder Band
2. "Forever" by Kari Jobe

**What Did You Read?**
Luke 10:25–37, The Good Samaritan

**What Did You Learn?**

_____

_____

_____

_____

_____

_____

**How Can You Apply What You Have Learned to Your Daily Life?**

_____

_____

_____

_____

_____

_____

**Prayer**

_____

_____

_____

_____

_____

## Songs for Worship

1. "What a Beautiful Name" by Hillsong
2. "Build My Life" by Housefires

**What Did You Read?**
Luke 15:1–32, Lost and Found

**What Did You Learn?**

_____

_____

_____

_____

_____

_____

**How Can You Apply What You Have Learned to Your Daily Life?**

_____

_____

_____

_____

_____

_____

**Prayer**

_____

_____

_____

_____

_____

## *Songs for Worship* ———————————————————

1. "Reckless Love" by Cory Asbury
2. "Do It Again" by Elevation Worship

**What Did You Read?**
Matthew 14:22–36, Walking on Water

**What Did You Learn?**

———————————————————————
———————————————————————
———————————————————————
———————————————————————
———————————————————————

**How Can You Apply What You Have Learned to Your Daily Life?**

———————————————————————
———————————————————————
———————————————————————
———————————————————————
———————————————————————

**Prayer**

———————————————————————
———————————————————————
———————————————————————
———————————————————————
———————————————————————

## Weekly Reflection

What were three *big* wins for the week?

1. _____
2. _____
3. _____

What were some of the game-changing lessons learned?

_____
_____
_____
_____

What are you grateful for this week?

_____
_____
_____
_____

How have you connected with others this week?

_____
_____
_____
_____

What has been your prayer focus and why?

_____
_____
_____
_____

# Notes and Ideas

## CHAPTER 5

# RESCUED

For fifteen days, Darlene lay unable to move, trapped under a piece of metal in four feet of rubble after the 7.0 earthquake struck Port-au-Prince, Haiti. Just moments before, the sixteen-year-old had been showering in her cousin's home after a normal day without a care in the world. Now, nearing death, she continued to cry out for help from those who passed by. Thankfully, a man heard her groaning, and within hours, rescuers dug a four-foot-deep and two-and-a-half-foot-wide trench and pulled her to safety. It was a miracle Darlene and her loved ones will never forget.

We have all at one time or another been covered by the rubble of our mistakes and failures. We have all sinned and fallen short of God's standards (Romans 3:23). Thankfully, God hears our cries for help and rescues us. If not for His grace, we would still be lying there in the aftershock of our own earthquakes of life. We no longer remain buried alive and trapped in sin. We are living miracles, just like Darlene.

Paul wrote a letter to the believers in Colossi and encouraged them with these words: "For he has rescued us from the dominion of darkness and brought us into the kingdom of the Son he loves, in whom we have redemption, the forgiveness of sins" (Colossians 1:13–14).

These two verses continue Paul's thought using the analogy of Israel inheriting the Promised Land (Exodus 6:6; 12:27). The story of the exodus demonstrates how God rescued His people from the slavery in Egypt and led them to the Promised Land. The Israelites were rescued, delivered from danger, saved from slavery, and given a clean start with an abundant inheritance. The word *redemption* means "to buy back" or "to save from captivity by paying a ransom."[1]

What a descriptive picture of what God has done for us! Like the man who heard Darlene's moans as he passed by, Jesus has heard our cry for mercy. We who were slaves to sin have been rescued and redeemed by the sacrifice of Christ on the cross. We are no longer slaves but sons and daughters—heirs of the heavenly kingdom. Our sins have been paid for, and now we simply need to trust in Jesus (Romans 8:15–17). This is the journey of our growing faith.

Can you think back to the day Jesus rescued you? For me, it wasn't anything dramatic. I was blessed to grow up in a Christian home. Weekly church attendance and conversations about God were the norm. Early on in my teen years, however, I realized that religious rituals didn't satisfy. My parents' faith was more condemning and confining than the freedom and fullness of life they preached. That wasn't their fault though. I had to own that. I had to make faith personal. It had to be *my* faith. I needed to have my own personal relationship with Jesus.

I remember asking Jesus to make it personal between us. That twelve-year-old version of me asked to be rescued from religion so we could have a relationship. I no longer just wanted to know the stories in the Bible. I wanted to become part of the story of God's destiny for humanity.

What is your story? What were you like before God rescued you? How did you come to know Jesus? Take a moment and jot down the details below. Thank Him for responding to your cry for help.

_____

_____

_____

_____

_____

_____

_____

_____

_____

_____

_____

_____

_____

_____

_____

_____

_____

_____

_____

_____

_____

_____

_____

_____

_____

_____

_____

_____

## *Songs for Worship*

1. "Good Good Father" by Chris Tomlin
2. "Blood So Beautiful" by Christ for the Nations

**What Did You Read?**
John 19:1–42, The Crucifixion

**What Did You Learn?**

_____

_____

_____

_____

_____

_____

**How Can You Apply What You Have Learned to Your Daily Life?**

_____

_____

_____

_____

_____

_____

**Prayer**

_____

_____

_____

_____

_____

_____

## Songs for Worship

1. "Rattle" by Elevation Worship
2. "Yes I Will" by Vertical Worship

**What Did You Read?**
John 20:1–21:25, The Resurrection

**What Did You Learn?**

_____
_____
_____
_____
_____
_____

**How Can You Apply What You Have Learned to Your Daily Life?**

_____
_____
_____
_____
_____
_____

**Prayer**

_____
_____
_____
_____
_____

# Songs for Worship

1. "Death Was Arrested" by North Pointe Worship
2. "Where You Are" by Leeland

**What Did You Read?**
Acts 1:1–11, The Ascension

**What Did You Learn?**

_____

_____

_____

_____

_____

**How Can You Apply What You Have Learned to Your Daily Life?**

_____

_____

_____

_____

_____

**Prayer**

_____

_____

_____

_____

_____

## Songs for Worship

1. "Holy Spirit" by Bryan & Katie Torwalt
2. "Rain" by Noel Robinson and Leeland

**What Did You Read?**
Acts 2:1–47, The Day of Pentecost

**What Did You Learn?**

_____
_____
_____
_____
_____
_____

**How Can You Apply What You Have Learned to Your Daily Life?**

_____
_____
_____
_____
_____
_____

**Prayer**

_____
_____
_____
_____
_____

## *Songs for Worship*

1. "Defender" by Upper Room
2. "Out of Hiding" by Steffany Gretzinger

**What Did You Read?**
Acts 3:1–4:37, Growth and Persecution

**What Did You Learn?**

_____

_____

_____

_____

_____

**How Can You Apply What You Have Learned to Your Daily Life?**

_____

_____

_____

_____

_____

**Prayer**

_____

_____

_____

_____

_____

## Songs for Worship

1. "Nothing Else" by Cody Carnes
2. "Revelation Song" by Kari Jobe

**What Did You Read?**
Acts 6:8–8:8, The First Martyr

**What Did You Learn?**

_____
_____
_____
_____
_____
_____

**How Can You Apply What You Have Learned to Your Daily Life?**

_____
_____
_____
_____
_____
_____

**Prayer**

_____
_____
_____
_____
_____

# Weekly Reflection

What were three *big* wins for the week?

1. _____
2. _____
3. _____

What were some of the game-changing lessons learned?

_____
_____
_____
_____

What are you grateful for this week?

_____
_____
_____
_____

How have you connected with others this week?

_____
_____
_____
_____

What has been your prayer focus and why?

_____
_____
_____
_____

## Notes and Ideas

CHAPTER 6

# TRANSFORMATION: CHOOSE TO CHANGE

After three consecutive championships in the NBA, Michael Jordan changed his mind about what sport he wanted to play professionally. He decided to walk away from basketball and try his hand at baseball. I was beyond heartbroken. The world joined me in mourning until, two long years later, Michael changed his mind again and returned to the Bulls' starting lineup. That year, he led his team to a record-breaking 72–10 season and three more consecutive championships. Others in professional sports, such as Brett Favre, have had similar experiences of coming in and out of retirement, but unfortunately, he didn't have the same measure of success.

Consider how many times you have changed your mind about various things in life. Many of us have changed our minds concerning our careers, relationships—even our hairstyles. Sometimes, though, our change of mind is really a change of heart. We decide on a course of action, and then because of our passions and deep desires, we end up going another direction.

Maybe we aren't that different from Michael Jordan or Brett Favre. We have "retired" from our old life when Jesus rescued us from the penalty of sin. On the day we decided to make Jesus the Lord of our lives, it's as if we started a new career of sorts. That change of heart was the beginning of a process of transformation that will continue until we reach heaven. This change of heart is an everyday decision to live our lives to please God rather than ourselves. The biblical term is "sanctification"—a separation from sin and a setting apart unto God. It begins when we give Jesus control of our lives, and it progresses as we continue to believe and submit to the leading of the Holy Spirit.

One of the best biblical examples of this can be found in the life of Saul of Tarsus, who later became known as Paul. Saul was one of the most religiously educated and revered people of his day. Being religious, however, doesn't mean you're good. He was actually "breathing out murderous threats against the Lord's disciples" (Acts 9:1). He was having Christians imprisoned and killed.

God had a bigger plan for Saul just like He has a plan for you and me. God confronted him as he traveled to his next gig on the road to Damascus. God knocked him off his high horse (literally) and blinded him with the truth (also literally). That road trip brought Saul to a life-altering change of heart. Rescued and healed, Saul became Paul, and he changed from the most feared persecutor of Christians to the most respected promoter of Christianity. He traveled hundreds of miles and planted numerous churches, and his writings comprise a large portion of the New Testament.

In his writing to the church, Paul challenges believers to set their hearts and minds on things above, not on earthly things (Colossians 3:1–2). He indicates that our change is both an intellectual decision and an emotional one. We decide to follow Christ based not only on logic ("I want the gift of eternal life") but also on passion ("I want to love God in return"). Setting our hearts and minds on things above is our part in the relationship. He rescues; we are transformed.

Grab your Bible and read the first eleven verses of Colossians 3. You will discover the change of heart and mind Paul said we need to make. Put to death sexual immorality, impurity, lust, evil desires, and greed. Rid yourself of anger, rage, malice, slander, and filthy talk; and don't lie. This isn't necessarily an exhaustive list, but it's a great place to start.

Christ has rescued us, and these things should no longer be part of our lifestyles. Put those things to death. Have a funeral. Bury them and say goodbye. We take off our old selves—those old habits—and we put on a new identity, "which is being renewed in knowledge in the image of its Creator" (v. 10). It's like taking off our old Members Only jacket from junior high and putting on a new Patagonia nano puff coat. It's a huge change.

Paul describes this change more deeply in Romans 12:2: "Do not conform to the pattern of this world but be transformed by the renewing of your mind. Then you will be able to test and approve what God's will is—his good, pleasing and perfect will."

The Greek word for "transform" is *metamorphoo*. This is where we get our English word *metamorphosis*, which can mean (1) "the process of transformation from an immature form to an adult form in two or more distinct stages" or (2) "a complete change in form or nature" (*Concise Oxford English Dictionary*). A perfect example is how a caterpillar transforms into a butterfly. That change is a force of nature.

Transformation is a choice. It's an intentional decision to change from the inside out. Transforming by the renewing of your mind means you change your manner of thinking. To renew your mind, you must remove your old patterns of thinking as the world thinks and replace them with the standards laid out in the Bible. How we think molds our behaviors. "As a man thinks, so he is" (Proverbs 23:7). Those behaviors then shape the passions and desires of our hearts.

A renewed mind will result in a transformed life. You will be transformed from a person of selfish patterns and practices to a person of sacrifice and service. You will live to please and honor God in all you do. It's a choice you willfully make every day to think and act differently.

Here are some additional scriptures you can read this week to further your understanding of this process of transformation: Ephesians 4:17–24; 2 Corinthians 5:17.

Are there patterns in your former life that still need to be "put to death"? In what way can you symbolically have a funeral and bury them for good?

_____

_____

_____

_____

The heart is the seat of our emotions, and the mind is the seat of our intellect. Giving our lives to Jesus needs to include a radical change of our minds and hearts. God does His part of saving us, and we do our part of separating ourselves from the world. We replace our old patterns with new ones based on God's truth found in the Bible. That acquired knowledge then leads to a heart change exhibited by our actions. We not only "take off" and "put to death" our former life, but we also must "put on the new self." We must see ourselves as having a whole new identity—a new heart, meaning a new set of passions; and a new mind, which includes new desires and a new way of thinking.

What differences do you see in your life since you put your faith in Jesus? How have others noticed these changes?

_____

_____

_____

_____

What choices are you intentionally making to move forward in your change of mind and heart?

_____

_____

_____

_____

_____

_____

_____

_____

What one thing can you do today to begin the process of changing?

_____

_____

_____

_____

_____

_____

_____

_____

## *Songs for Worship*

1. "Word of God Speak" by MercyMe
2. "New Wine" by Hillsong Worship

**What Did You Read?**
Acts 8:26–40, Sharing the Word

**What Did You Learn?**

_____
_____
_____
_____
_____
_____

**How Can You Apply What You Have Learned to Your Daily Life?**

_____
_____
_____
_____
_____
_____

**Prayer**

_____
_____
_____
_____
_____
_____

# Songs for Worship

1. "Better Word" by Leeland
2. "Great I Am" by New Life Worship

**What Did You Read?**
Acts 10:1–11:18, Good News for All

**What Did You Learn?**

_____
_____
_____
_____
_____
_____

**How Can You Apply What You Have Learned to Your Daily Life?**

_____
_____
_____
_____
_____
_____

**Prayer**

_____
_____
_____
_____
_____

## *Songs for Worship* ─────────────────

1. "No Longer Slaves" by Bethel Music
2. "Be a Victory" by Elevation Worship

**What Did You Read?**
Romans 8:1–39, More Than Conquerors

**What Did You Learn?**

_____
_____
_____
_____
_____
_____

**How Can You Apply What You Have Learned to Your Daily Life?**

_____
_____
_____
_____
_____
_____

**Prayer**

_____
_____
_____
_____
_____
_____

## Songs for Worship

1. "Here Again" by Elevation Worship
2. "Holy Ground" by Passion and Melodie Malone

**What Did You Read?**
Galatians 5:16–6:10, The Fruit of the Spirit

**What Did You Learn?**

_____

_____

_____

_____

_____

**How Can You Apply What You Have Learned to Your Daily Life?**

_____

_____

_____

_____

_____

**Prayer**

_____

_____

_____

_____

_____

## Songs for Worship

1. "Break Every Chain" by Jesus Culture
2. "The More I Seek You" by Klaus and Kari Jobe

**What Did You Read?**
Ephesians 6:10–20, The Armor of God

**What Did You Learn?**

_____

_____

_____

_____

_____

_____

**How Can You Apply What You Have Learned to Your Daily Life?**

_____

_____

_____

_____

_____

_____

**Prayer**

_____

_____

_____

_____

_____

## *Songs for Worship*

1. "Raise a Hallelujah" by Bethel Music
2. "Glorious Day" by Passion and Kristian Stanfill

**What Did You Read?**
Philippians 4:2–9, Rejoice in the Lord

**What Did You Learn?**

_____

_____

_____

_____

_____

**How Can You Apply What You Have Learned to Your Daily Life?**

_____

_____

_____

_____

_____

**Prayer**

_____

_____

_____

_____

_____

## Weekly Reflection _____

What were three *big* wins for the week?

1. _____
2. _____
3. _____

What were some of the game-changing lessons learned?

_____
_____
_____
_____

What are you grateful for this week?

_____
_____
_____
_____

How have you connected with others this week?

_____
_____
_____
_____

What has been your prayer focus and why?

_____
_____
_____
_____

## Notes and Ideas

# CHAPTER 7

# GOING PUBLIC

When you hear the phrase "going public," you may think of when an organization decides to become a publicly traded company in the stock exchange in hopes of expanding and raising capital. Maybe you think of it as when a government official makes public his or her desire to run for a higher public office like the presidency. In similar fashion, when we take the next step of being baptized by immersion in water according to scripture, we declare to the world that we have decided to give our lives to Christ.

When we read Matthew 28:19, we can see the importance that Jesus placed on water baptism as part of the process of growing as a follower of Jesus (a believer, disciple). Jesus said, "Therefore go and make disciples of all nations, baptizing them in the name of the Father and of the Son and of the Holy Spirit." Our responsibility as a disciple is to be baptized and to baptize others. This *going public* isn't a ritual but more of a rite of passage. It's a testimony of what Jesus did for the world and how His sacrifice has changed your life.

John the Baptist is the first one seen in the Bible baptizing believers (Matthew 3:6). Then on the Day of Pentecost in Acts 2:38, Peter, under the direction of the Holy Spirit, commands his listeners to "repent and be baptized, every one of you." Even Jesus was baptized as an example for us to follow. The word used most in the Bible to represent baptism is *baptizo*, which means to dip completely or immerse. Water baptism is a ceremony in which a person is submerged, immersed, or dunked into and under water. Mark 1:5 gives the same description.

Baptism is a physical picture of a spiritual reality. It is an outward sign of an inward change. We are buried with Christ in baptism and raised to walk in a brand-new life. The meaning and significance of baptism are forever connected to Jesus's death and resurrection. It is an *act* of obedience and a sign of repentance that *acts* as an object lesson connected to the life, death, and resurrection of the Son of God.

If you were sprinkled or had water poured over your head as a child in church, that was your parents committing you to God, and that is a precious display of their love and desire for you. But now as an adult, you need to decide for yourself to obey God's command to be baptized in water.

You may ask, "Do I need to be baptized to be a Christian?" Mark 16:16 says, "Whoever believes and is baptized will be saved, but whoever does not believe will be condemned." The issue is belief, not baptism. The relationship of salvation to baptism is the same as salvation to obedience. If we have decided to make Jesus the Lord of our lives, we are "saved," and we will want to obey Him. So if we are believers, Christians, and disciples, then our lives should demonstrate that through works of obedience; faith without works is dead faith (James 2:14). So if you're saved, you will want to be baptized.

Baptism is a ceremony in which a person has professed his or her faith in Jesus Christ and in obedience is immersed in water, therefore identifying himself or herself to Christ—the death of his or her old life and the birth of the *new* and *improved* life. If you haven't yet taken the opportunity to be baptized in water, contact your church as soon as possible. I am certain they would be honored to help you "go public" with your faith.

If you have already been baptized in water since committing your life to Jesus, explain briefly what that experience meant to you. What church were you connected with at the time? When did it take place? Who baptized you? Who was there to celebrate with you?

_____

_____

_____

_____

_____

_____

_____

_____

_____

_____

_____

_____

_____

_____

_____

_____

_____

_____

_____

_____

_____

_____

_____

## Songs for Worship

1. "Faithful" by Erik Nieder
2. "Yes and Amen" by Housefires

**What Did You Read?**
1 Timothy 3:1–16, Church Leadership

**What Did You Learn?**

_____

_____

_____

_____

_____

**How Can You Apply What You Have Learned to Your Daily Life?**

_____

_____

_____

_____

_____

**Prayer**

_____

_____

_____

_____

_____

# Songs for Worship

1. "Authority" by Elevation Worship
2. "Simple Gospel" by United Pursuit

**What Did You Read?**
2 Timothy 3:10–4:8, Authority of Scripture

**What Did You Learn?**

_____

_____

_____

_____

_____

_____

**How Can You Apply What You Have Learned to Your Daily Life?**

_____

_____

_____

_____

_____

_____

**Prayer**

_____

_____

_____

_____

_____

## Songs for Worship

1. "When You Walk into the Room" by Bryan & Katie Torwalt
2. "How Beautiful" by Mosaic MSC

**What Did You Read?**
Romans 8:1–39, More Than Conquerors

**What Did You Learn?**

_____
_____
_____
_____
_____

**How Can You Apply What You Have Learned to Your Daily Life?**

_____
_____
_____
_____
_____

**Prayer**

_____
_____
_____
_____

# Songs for Worship

1. "This Love" by Housefires
2. "No Fear In Love" by Steffany Gretzinger

**What Did You Read?**
1 Corinthians 13:1–13, The Secrets of True Love

**What Did You Learn?**

_____

_____

_____

_____

_____

_____

**How Can You Apply What You Have Learned to Your Daily Life?**

_____

_____

_____

_____

_____

_____

**Prayer**

_____

_____

_____

_____

_____

## Songs for Worship

1. "Run to the Father" by Cody Carnes
2. "Faith and Wonder" by Upper Room

**What Did You Read?**
1 Peter 1:1–2:12, A Living Hope

**What Did You Learn?**

_____

_____

_____

_____

_____

**How Can You Apply What You Have Learned to Your Daily Life?**

_____

_____

_____

_____

_____

**Prayer**

_____

_____

_____

_____

_____

## Songs for Worship

1. "Another in the Fire" by Hillsong Worship
2. "Reckless Love" by Cory Asbury

**What Did You Read?**
1 John 3:11–4:21, Love for Others

**What Did You Learn?**

_____

_____

_____

_____

_____

_____

**How Can You Apply What You Have Learned to Your Daily Life?**

_____

_____

_____

_____

_____

_____

**Prayer**

_____

_____

_____

_____

_____

## *Weekly Reflection* ——————————

What were three *big* wins for the week?

1. _____
2. _____
3. _____

What were some of the game-changing lessons learned?

_____
_____
_____
_____

What are you grateful for this week?

_____
_____
_____
_____

How have you connected with others this week?

_____
_____
_____
_____

What has been your prayer focus and why?

_____
_____
_____
_____

## Notes and Ideas

CHAPTER 8

# THE PERFECT STORM

The *Andrea Gail* was a seventy-two-foot commercial fishing boat captained by thirty-seven-year-old Frank Tyne Jr. She began her final voyage on September 20, 1991. Departing from Gloucester Harbor, Massachusetts, she was bound for the Grand Banks of Newfoundland off the coast of eastern Canada. Poor fishing and a malfunctioning ice machine moved the captain and crew to set course for home on October 26 despite weather reports of dangerous conditions.

The boat and her crew were over 162 miles from shore when they last radioed in their position. "She's comin' on, boys, and she's comin' on strong." The *Andrea Gail* was overcome by the "perfect storm" shortly after and was never heard from again.

Journalist Sebastian Junger coined the "perfect storm" moniker after a conversation with meteorologist Robert Case, in which Case described the convergence of weather conditions as being "perfect" for the formation of such a storm. Basically, an extratropical storm collided with Hurricane Grace and powered up to become a cyclone.

It was kind of like when Pac-Man eats a power pellet and gets supercharged to eat the ghosts.

Having lived in Florida, Rhode Island, and now Southeast Texas, I have a vivid understanding of storms. Hurricane season is on our calendars from June 1 through November 30. When you live in the path storms travel, you tend to be aware of the predictive models, alert to up-to-date weather reports, and prepared for the worst. Makes sense, right?

Shortly after moving to Florida, my wife and I drove a few towns over for a date. We did some shopping, grabbed something to eat, and then headed home. We were driving on this secluded county road when suddenly the weather shifted. The sun disappeared, and a wall of clouds came out of nowhere and raced toward us. In an instant, sheets of rain came down so heavy that we were forced to stop dead in our tracks. I turned on our hazard lights and hoped no one would hit us from behind. Then as quickly as the storm started, it stopped. We took the Florida weather more seriously after that.

I think you would agree that as natural as hurricanes are, so are the various storms in life. There are seasons in life just as in nature, where the unexpected happens. Circumstances, relationships, health, and finances are constantly on a collision course that warrants us to always be aware, alert, and prepared for anything. It may not be the perfect storm of 1991, but the effects of divorce, loss of a job, the passing of a loved one, the rebellion of a child, or the pain of a returning addiction can be destructive and debilitating.

Can we predict storms? Can we prevent them? Can we survive them? How much damage will they cause? What can we learn from the storms we experience? These are questions the book of James helps to answer.

James was written to the Christian Jews scattered all over the Greek-Roman Empire. The early church had its problems just like any other organization. They had some storms that needed navigating, and James was the man of the hour. Christians then, just like today, were facing temptations to sin, dealing with political unrest, struggling with favoritism and prejudice, competing for a position, battling worldliness, and failing to live by what they professed to believe.

What storms are you facing right now?

_____

_____

_____

_____

September 11, 2001, brought war to our shores. There are so many things etched into my memory from that day, but one positive outcome was the resolve of the American people to join together in unity, to never give up, and to rebuild what had been torn down. Even thirteen years later, our country remained proud and vigilant as we opened One World Trade Center, with its spire reaching 1,776 feet in the air, very specifically reminding us of the independence we declared in 1776. This building is the tallest in the United States and is a constant reminder that we are still standing strong in our freedom.

Another building astonishes me—not because of how tall it is but rather because of how deep its foundation goes. The Petronas Twin Towers of Malaysia stand 1,483 feet tall, but their foundations are the deepest in the world at nearly 400 feet. Their foundations are as tall as the Statue of Liberty or a thirty-three-story building!

A deep foundation transfers the weight of a building down to the earth. Before ever building up, construction teams must build down. You have to go down to the bedrock, the layer of solid rock below the soil. If you want to reach new heights, you must first dig deep. That is where you find stability.

Here is how the *Andrea Gail* and the Petronas Towers tie together. Let's look back at when Jesus was delivering the Sermon on the Mount. He had touched on so many topics and principles, and now was bringing His message to a close. In His usual fashion, He shared a parable. This one was centered on a wise and foolish builder and speaks to both storms and foundations.

> Therefore, everyone who hears these words of mine
> and puts them into practice is like a wise man who
> built his house on the rock. The rain came down,
> the streams rose, and the winds blew and beat upon
> that house; yet it did not fall, because it had its
> foundation on the rock. *But* everyone who hears
> these words of mine and does not put them into
> practice is like a foolish man who built his house
> on sand. The rain came down, the streams rose,
> and the winds blew and beat against the house,
> and it fell with a great crash. (Matthew 7:24–27,
> emphasis added)

You may have heard it said that everyone is heading into a storm, coming out of a storm, or preparing for a storm. Jesus explained that both the wise and foolish builders faced the same three elements of the storm: rain falling, streams rising, and wind blowing. Some may feel this is unfair. Why should I face storms in life when I am doing everything I know to do to live right? But do we really want to talk about what's fair when the sinless Son of God gave His life so we could be rescued from the wrath of God? That will make you think.

What we tend to overlook is that the focal point of the story isn't the storm but the builder's foundation. But before we get to the foundation, let's look at what the storm brings to the party.

The first element is the rain falling. When it rains, we get wet, and when we get wet, we become uncomfortable. Sound familiar? For our house, however, the rain exposes weaknesses in areas that have flaws and have been improperly sealed, such as the siding, windows, and roof. These exposures then allow for leaks, which can cause structural damage and weaken the foundation.

When the rain refuses to let up, the streams begin to rise, overtake their banks, and spill over into the streets. When streams flood, they tend to carry stuff away that isn't secured, and it loosens the already-weakened foundation.

Finally, the wind blows and beats against the house. Wind can cause some pretty substantial damage. I've seen the wind pick up trees, patio furniture, and trampolines, and throw them up against a neighbor's home three doors down. Gusts of wind can also blow out windows and tear roofs right off. The wind is powerful and unpredictable.

When you couple that force of the wind with the rain and the streams that have exposed the home's weaknesses and loosened the failing foundation, it can utterly destroy the whole structure and anyone inside. Talk to anyone who has lived through a hurricane, tornado, or tropical cyclone, and he or she will passionately tell you about the destructive forces of a storm. Then the person will give you a list of things you need to do to be prepared.

Jesus may not have been a meteorologist like Al Roker or an architect like Frank Lloyd Wright, but remember, He was a present participant in creation. He spoke plainly and logically about common truths His listeners were very aware of. Jesus shows a progression of the storm in exposing, weakening, loosening, and potentially destroying the house.

Here is the life-altering point of the parable. This progression of destruction is only one of the possible outcomes. All of us have storms in our lives, but they don't have to destroy us. We can prepare for the storm by digging a deep foundation.

The difference between the wise and foolish builder is the foundation of obedience and faith. Hearers and active doers of the Word can stand strong in the storm. Those who hear but don't act on the truth will suffer the collapse of their faith and lives. It's not rocket science. It's hard work, but it is very attainable.

James tells us to consider it pure joy when storms come because the testing of our faith actually produces perseverance (James 1:2–3). It's as if the storm not only proves our faith but also makes our foundation even stronger with deeper roots. Our destiny is directly connected to our commitment to obey His Word. It's the true test of our faith (James 1:22–25).

Luke also records this parable of Jesus but uses more descriptive language when talking about the wise builder. Luke said that he "dug down deep and laid a foundation on rock," but that house couldn't be shaken (Luke 6:48).

Personally, I want to be a wise builder, and I'm sure you do as well. So what do we need to do?

We need to *examine our foundation!* What is the foundation of my life built on? Am I building on my social standing with followers on Facebook, Instagram, or TikTok? Is my life built on my financial status by how much I make or how much I can buy and accumulate? Is my foundation built on how smart I can be or how up to date I am with politics and current events? Or is my foundation built on faith in Christ alone? He needs to be our bedrock.

A second thing we can do is *look back* at the most recent storm in our lives. We probably don't have to look back too far. Look back at that storm and answer honestly; were you shaken? Did it expose some weaknesses? Was your foundation loosened, or was something carried off? Did your house fall apart altogether?

A third thing we need to do is *dig down deep*. Building a foundation is labor intensive and time consuming. Daily practice of spiritual disciplines is the bedrock of our foundation of faith. Daily disciplines are the tools that allow us to dig deep. We need to get past the topsoil. Dig deep into God's Word. Learn His character, His compassion, and His commands for daily life. Dig into prayer and practice silence and solitude, where you can listen for His voice and be led by His Spirit. Every time we worship, journal, fast, serve, and encourage others, we dig a little deeper.

Building a foundation isn't noticeable to anyone else. The incredible skyscraper will never be admired and appreciated until the unnoticed, underground deep digging is done and the foundation is laid. Digging that deep foundation is what sets us up for longevity and success. The deeper you dig, the more firm the foundation will be. When life happens, trials come, and storms hit, we can stand strong and be unshakable and immovable.

If we want to reach new heights, we need to dig deep. We need to examine our foundation, evaluate how we are handling storms, and engage in spiritual disciplines.

How deep is your foundation, and what is it being built on?

_____

_____

_____

_____

_____

_____

How have you been handling your storms? What have been the results?

_____

_____

_____

_____

_____

_____

How would you rate your current spiritual habits?

_____

_____

_____

_____

_____

_____

## *Songs for Worship*

1. "Here Is Heaven" by Elevation Worship
2. "This Is a Move" by Brandon Lakes

**What Did You Read?**
James 1:1–18, Testing to Triumph

**What Did You Learn?**

_____

_____

_____

_____

_____

**How Can You Apply What You Have Learned to Your Daily Life?**

_____

_____

_____

_____

_____

**Prayer**

_____

_____

_____

_____

_____

## Songs for Worship

1. "Yes I Will" by Vertical Worship
2. "Peace Be Still" by Lauren Daigle

**What Did You Read?**
James 1:19–25; Mirror, Mirror on the Wall

**What Did You Learn?**

_____

_____

_____

_____

_____

**How Can You Apply What You Have Learned to Your Daily Life?**

_____

_____

_____

_____

_____

**Prayer**

_____

_____

_____

_____

_____

## Songs for Worship

1. "Wait for You" by Leeland
2. "Goodness of God" by Bethel Music

**What Did You Read?**

James 2:1–13, The Titanic Syndrome

**What Did You Learn?**

_____

_____

_____

_____

_____

_____

**How Can You Apply What You Have Learned to Your Daily Life?**

_____

_____

_____

_____

_____

**Prayer**

_____

_____

_____

_____

_____

## Songs for Worship

1. "After You" by Upper Room
2. "Spirit of the Living God" by Vertical Music

**What Did You Read?**
James 2:14–26, I See Dead People

**What Did You Learn?**

_____

_____

_____

_____

_____

**How Can You Apply What You Have Learned to Your Daily Life?**

_____

_____

_____

_____

_____

**Prayer**

_____

_____

_____

_____

_____

## *Songs for Worship*

1. "Lean Back" by Capital City Music
2. "First Love Fire" by Leeland

**What Did You Read?**
James 3:1–12; Open Mouth, Insert Foot

**What Did You Learn?**

_____
_____
_____
_____
_____
_____

**How Can You Apply What You Have Learned to Your Daily Life?**

_____
_____
_____
_____
_____
_____

**Prayer**

_____
_____
_____
_____
_____
_____

## Songs for Worship

1. "Jesus You Alone" by Highlands Worship
2. "To Worship You I Live" by Israel Houghton

**What Did You Read?**
James 4:1–12, Get Serious

**What Did You Learn?**

_____

_____

_____

_____

_____

**How Can You Apply What You Have Learned to Your Daily Life?**

_____

_____

_____

_____

_____

_____

**Prayer**

_____

_____

_____

_____

_____

## Weekly Reflection

What were three *big* wins for the week?

1. _____
2. _____
3. _____

What were some of the game-changing lessons learned?

_____
_____
_____
_____

What are you grateful for this week?

_____
_____
_____
_____

How have you connected with others this week?

_____
_____
_____
_____

What has been your prayer focus and why?

_____
_____
_____
_____

## Notes and Ideas

CHAPTER 9

# PAY ATTENTION

Learning how to drive was a long, drawn-out process for me. If memory serves me correctly, we had only one car at this point. It was a mideighties Renault Encore with a manual transmission. This super-economical car was uncool for a teenager, but I had to learn. My legally blind father was the first to attempt teaching me. What could possibly go wrong?

My dad took me a few blocks down from our house into a church parking lot for my first lesson. We switched seats, and he walked me through the process of using the clutch, shifting the gears, and keeping my hands on the wheel and my eyes on the road. The training was a bit overwhelming, but I was so excited to get on the road.

Learning how to drive is no easy task. There are so many details to process and so much potential for danger. Even our little French-made seventy-eight-horsepower hatchback could cause some serious harm and damage if not used properly. You probably have some interesting stories of your own that you could share.

It didn't take long for my father to lose patience with my failed attempts to just pull out into first gear. I rode the clutch, stalled out, and bucked that poor car like breaking in a bronco. I don't think we even moved ten feet before my dad said the lesson was over and asked me to get out. He drove me home, and that was my last lesson from him. I'm glad we were only a few blocks from home because neither of us spoke a word.

The following Saturday, my mom took me to my old elementary school parking lot to give me a chance to redeem myself. She drove in a circle and demonstrated for me how to use the clutch, shift gears, and then slowly give the car some gas to increase the speed. The directions really seemed so easy. I could do this.

Well, to my young and overconfident surprise, I still struggled. I was anything but smooth while trying to get it into first gear. I nearly gave us both whiplash several times. You could even smell the clutch burning as I overcompensated because I was so afraid of stalling it for the hundredth time. My second driving lesson ended abruptly once again—not because of my mom's lack of patience but because I had jammed the gear box. We had to get the car towed and repaired.

My brother Dave also had a hand in teaching me how to drive. He actually gave me my first opportunity to drive on a highway. We were on our way home from a job I had just helped him with about thirty-five miles out of town in the Scranton area. We stopped at a convenience store for some snacks, and as we walked back to the car, he announced that I was driving home.

I was as nervous as I was excited, but there was no way I was turning down the offer. He gave me a quick rundown of the car's features and said he was going to take a nap. I eagerly pulled onto Interstate 81, both hands white knuckled on the steering wheel. I kept the speedometer at fifty-five and stayed perfectly in the center of the right lane. This was driving … until it almost wasn't.

We were about ten minutes into our drive home, and Dave was all but snoring as he peacefully napped in the passenger seat. I hadn't yet touched my coffee or Tastykake I had bought earlier, and I could hear them calling to me. There was steam escaping from the coffee as it sat there in the cup holder. The smell was intoxicating. Surely I could just grab it and take a sip while I was driving, right? I mean, everyone does it. I'd watched my brother do the same thing on the drive to our job site.

As I reached for my coffee, my mouth watered in anticipation of that first sip. My gratification was sadly interrupted as my brother's Spidey senses tingled, and he snapped out of his sleep. "Pay attention, or you're going to get us both killed," he exclaimed. He didn't yell; that wasn't his thing, but he definitely said it with authority. He'd noticed that as my eyes and my hand went to pick up my coffee, my other hand followed in the same direction, causing the car to drift off the road.

I learned a valuable lesson that day. We tend to drift in the direction of the things that have our attention. An even-deeper application would be, What gets our attention determines our direction and ultimately, our destination. That desire for a sip of my coffee nearly ended in disaster because it had caused me to drift in the wrong direction.

I would imagine that we've all had similar experiences while driving. Hopefully, it wasn't from trying to text while driving, but maybe it was checking out a car, looking at a billboard, or even daydreaming. It can be a scary moment, and maybe you've even had an accident because of it.

Beyond the highway, we have other attention grabbers that distract us and cause us to drift in a certain direction. For some, it could be a relationship, a hobby, an addiction, technology, entertainment, or a video game. It has happened to all of us, right? We are going about our lives, doing our own thing, enjoying life, and then all of a sudden, "Squirrel." We see something that distracts us like coffee, and we drift in the direction of our attention.

Can you remember hearing someone telling you to pay attention? I've personally heard it quite a bit from teachers, my parents, my brother Dave, and spiritual leaders. I've said the phrase myself at least a hundred times as a parent, youth pastor, coach, and friend.

To "pay attention" implies a price, a cost, a giving away of something of value. Perhaps it's the sense of loss that keeps us from paying attention. Maybe it's the fear of missing out (FOMO). It can also be the cost associated with paying attention to the *right* things that makes it difficult to follow through.

King David seemed to have the experience to understand this principle. He said, "Direct me in the path of your commands, for there I find delight. Turn my heart toward your statutes and not toward selfish gain. Turn my eyes away from worthless things; preserve my life according to your word" (Psalm 119:35–37). He was speaking metaphorically of the attention of his heart and eyes.

The author of Hebrews gives us a fitting challenge: "We must pay the most careful attention, therefore, to what we have heard, so that we do not drift away" (Hebrews 2:1). To his readers, it was a specific warning not to be diverted away from the teachings of Christ being the Son of God and supreme over the angels. But the challenge is for all believers to stay focused so we don't drift or get carried away in our attention to other things.

Like a good driver's education teacher, the author urges his readers to get their eyes back on the road so they don't end up in a ditch or worse. As my brother did for me, he lovingly yet authoritatively told me to pay attention. He was aware that as your attention goes, so goes your life.

Paul told his listeners to pay attention on many occasions. He told the Corinthians, "Be on your guard" (1 Corinthians 16:13). He had to tell the Galatians, "Pay careful attention to your own work" (Galatians 6:4 NLT). To the Ephesians he said, "Be very careful, then, how you live—not as unwise but as wise" (Ephesians 5:15). Even the author of Hebrews reminded his readers to fix their eyes on Jesus (3:1). It's a message we need to hear with repetition.

Are you paying attention? If you haven't been, now is a great time to start. God cares about you and has a specific direction for your life (Jeremiah 29:11–13). What gets our attention determines our direction and ultimately our destination.

What has captured your attention and/or affections in a way that has distracted you from the things or people that deserve your attention? Have you considered that just because something isn't necessarily "bad," it can still cause you to drift away from what is better? Little things can quickly become big things as we drift off course from what God requires and desires for our lives. Take a moment now to journal about what God is speaking to your heart about your attention.

_____

_____

_____

_____

_____

_____

_____

_____

_____

_____

_____

_____

_____

_____

_____

_____

_____

_____

_____

## Songs for Worship

1. "Praise Before My Breakthrough" by Brian & Katie Torwalt
2. "Canvas and Clay" by Pat Barrett and Ben Smith

**What Did You Read?**
James 4:13–5:6, Plan Ahead

**What Did You Learn?**

_____
_____
_____
_____
_____
_____

**How Can You Apply What You Have Learned to Your Daily Life?**

_____
_____
_____
_____
_____
_____

**Prayer**

_____
_____
_____
_____
_____

## *Songs for Worship*

1. "Do It Again" by Elevation Worship
2. "Tremble" by Mosaic MSC

**What Did You Read?**
James 5:7–12, Stay the Course

**What Did You Learn?**

_____
_____
_____
_____
_____
_____

**How Can You Apply What You Have Learned to Your Daily Life?**

_____
_____
_____
_____
_____
_____

**Prayer**

_____
_____
_____
_____
_____
_____

## *Songs for Worship*

1. "Faithful Now" by Vertical Worship
2. "The Blessing" by Elevation Worship

**What Did You Read?**
James 5:13–20, Preventing an Epidemic

**What Did You Learn?**

_____

_____

_____

_____

_____

**How Can You Apply What You Have Learned to Your Daily Life?**

_____

_____

_____

_____

_____

**Prayer**

_____

_____

_____

_____

_____

## Songs for Worship

1. "Graves to Gardens" by Elevation Worship
2. "Hope Has a Name" by River Valley Worship

**What Did You Read?**
2 Timothy 2:1–26, Good Soldiers


**What Did You Learn?**

_____
_____
_____
_____
_____
_____

**How Can You Apply What You Have Learned to Your Daily Life?**

_____
_____
_____
_____
_____

**Prayer**

_____
_____
_____
_____
_____

## Songs for Worship

1. "Love Came Down" by Brian Johnson
2. "Wait upon the Lord" by Leeland

**What Did You Read?**

Revelation 1:1–20, A Voice and a Vision

**What Did You Learn?**

_____

_____

_____

_____

_____

**How Can You Apply What You Have Learned to Your Daily Life?**

_____

_____

_____

_____

_____

**Prayer**

_____

_____

_____

_____

_____

## Songs for Worship

1. "Lord I Need You" by Matt Maher
2. "Miracles" by Jesus Culture

**What Did You Read?**
Revelation 2:1–3:22, Message to the Churches

**What Did You Learn?**

_____
_____
_____
_____
_____
_____

**How Can You Apply What You Have Learned to Your Daily Life?**

_____
_____
_____
_____
_____
_____

**Prayer**

_____
_____
_____
_____
_____

## Weekly Reflection _____

What were three *big* wins for the week?

1. _____
2. _____
3. _____

What were some of the game-changing lessons learned?

_____
_____
_____
_____

What are you grateful for this week?

_____
_____
_____
_____

How have you connected with others this week?

_____
_____
_____
_____

What has been your prayer focus and why?

_____
_____
_____
_____

## Notes and Ideas

CHAPTER 10

# SIGNS OF DISCIPLESHIP

Take a moment and read John 15. To me the chapter is about some of the expectations of discipleship. It shows us what God expects from His disciples, what we can expect from the world as disciples, and what we can expect from God as His disciples.

How do you feel about expectations? How do the expectations you put on yourself differ from the expectations others put on you? Personally, I strive to surpass the expectations others hold me to. Do I always get there? No, but I enjoy the challenge (most of the time). However, far too often I fall short of the expectations I put on myself. Can you identify with that scenario?

For this discussion, let's focus on the first section of the chapter, verses 1–17. You probably noticed a vivid progression of bearing fruit. Jesus identifies Himself as the vine, His Father as the gardener, and we as the branches. The fruit to be produced is love demonstrated in obedience. It's love for God and others, and it reveals some explicit signs of discipleship.

The first sign is the responsibility of remaining. The whole discipleship process begins with, continues in, and ends as we remain in the life-giving and life-producing love and power of Jesus. The word *remain* means "to abide, continue, and last." Jesus uses the word eleven times in this section. I think He made His point pretty clear.

The second sign of discipleship is the progression of the production of fruit. Because we are part of the vine—Jesus—we have the ability to bear fruit. As we grow in His love, some fruit becomes more fruit, which then becomes much. Just keep in mind that part of discipleship is discipline. Any good arborist or vinedresser will prune trees and vines to remove lifeless branches and maintain maximum, high-quality grapes (fruit). This sometimes includes cutting away good branches to make room for better—bigger and sweeter grapes. It's as much about quantity as it is quality.

The third sign is what I call the math of multiplication. Verse 16 reads, "You did not choose me. I chose you. I appointed you to go and produce lasting (abiding) fruit, so that the Father will give you whatever you ask for, using my name" (NLT). The climax of remaining (abiding, continuing) as His disciples is when we leave a legacy of lasting fruit. It speaks of longevity and multiplication. Think about it. Fruit has within itself the seeds for more. One grape seed typically produces forty clusters of grapes, and those translate into ten bottles of wine.

A few years ago, the United Nations reported that globally, 45 percent of the fruit and vegetables produced are wasted. That's 3.7 trillion apples! (United Nations Twitter, January 26, 2013).[1] That could feed three hundred million people. For our fruit to be "lasting," we have to not only plant seeds but also remain part of the process to see those seeds produce their own fruit. We need to make sure the fruit isn't wasted. We now come full circle to become part of the progress of production for others.

We have been appointed and anointed to *go* and *produce* lasting fruit. That sounds a lot like Christ commissioning us to *go* and *make* disciples (Matthew 28:19). We take responsibility to remain; we progress in our production and embrace the math of multiplication. The fruit of our disciplined lives will plant seeds of discipleship in others that will multiply at exponential rates. This is love for God and others. This is obedience. These are the signs of discipleship.

What are the dead branches in your life that need to be cut off?

_____

_____

_____

_____

_____

Are there any things in your life that, though good, need to be cut off to make room for the better and best God wants for you?

_____

_____

_____

_____

How are you owning your own responsibility to remain?

_____

_____

_____

_____

What have you seen specifically as the benefits of your remaining?

_____

_____

_____

_____

## Songs for Worship

1. "Make Room" by Community Music
2. "Goodness of God" by One Sonic Society

**What Did You Read?**
Acts 9:1–31, Road to Damascus—Road to Redemption

**What Did You Learn?**

_____

_____

_____

_____

_____

**How Can You Apply What You Have Learned to Your Daily Life?**

_____

_____

_____

_____

_____

_____

**Prayer**

_____

_____

_____

_____

_____

## Songs for Worship

1. "Daybreak" by WorshipMob
2. "Spirit Break Out" by WorshipMob

**What Did You Read?**
Acts 13:1–14:28, Paul's First Missionary Journey

**What Did You Learn?**

_____

_____

_____

_____

_____

**How Can You Apply What You Have Learned to Your Daily Life?**

_____

_____

_____

_____

_____

**Prayer**

_____

_____

_____

_____

_____

*Songs for Worship*

"The Stand" by Upper Room

**What Did You Read?**
Acts 15:1–41, The Council at Jerusalem

**What Did You Learn?**

_____
_____
_____
_____
_____
_____

**How Can You Apply What You Have Learned to Your Daily Life?**

_____
_____
_____
_____
_____

**Prayer**

_____
_____
_____
_____
_____
_____

## Songs for Worship

"God I Look to You" by Bethel Worship

**What Did You Read?**
Acts 16:1–20:48, The Journey Continues

**What Did You Learn?**

_____

_____

_____

_____

_____

**How Can You Apply What You Have Learned to Your Daily Life?**

_____

_____

_____

_____

_____

**Prayer**

_____

_____

_____

_____

_____

## *Songs for Worship*

"You Are My Champion" by WorshipMob

**What Did You Read?**
Acts 25:1–28:31, Trip to Rome

**What Did You Learn?**

_____
_____
_____
_____
_____
_____

**How Can You Apply What You Have Learned to Your Daily Life?**

_____
_____
_____
_____
_____

**Prayer**

_____
_____
_____
_____
_____
_____

## *Songs for Worship*

"Here Again" by Rheva Henry and Bethel Worship

**What Did You Read?**

Matthew 28:19–20; Mark 16:15–18; Acts 1:8; The Great Commission

**What Did You Learn?**

_____

_____

_____

_____

_____

**How Can You Apply What You Have Learned to Your Daily Life?**

_____

_____

_____

_____

_____

**Prayer**

_____

_____

_____

_____

_____

## *Weekly Reflection* _____

What were three *big* wins for the week?

1. _____
2. _____
3. _____


What were some of the game-changing lessons learned?

_____
_____
_____
_____


What are you grateful for this week?

_____
_____
_____
_____


How have you connected with others this week?

_____
_____
_____
_____


What has been your prayer focus and why?

_____
_____
_____
_____

# Notes and Ideas

CHAPTER 11

# CHRIST'S LOVE COMPELS US

Some people just love to argue. Bring up politics, cultural hot buttons, or even sports, and they will jump on their bandwagon and do their best to convince you why their truth is reality while yours is fiction. Personally, I can talk for a long time about why Michael Jordan is the GOAT (greatest of all time) over Larry Bird, LeBron James, or any other wannabe. (I can have just as long of a conversation about why Tom Brady is the GOAT as well.) At the same time, I'm sure there are many of you reading who could have extended debates over Roe v. Wade, mask mandates, and the American Rescue Plan Act.

Having just read those statements, I know that I've triggered your emotions as well as your logic in a particular way. Truth be told, arguing is all about competition and comparing. The arguer is trying to win. Although the argumentative and persuasive person will use logic and evidence, the first is usually abrasive and judgmental, while the latter is most interested in moving the listener to action and next steps.

There are different driving forces behind our passion and motivation to be vocal about our opinions and beliefs. Our firsthand knowledge and personal experience should be at the top of that list. However, I'm sure we all have been guilty of jumping on a bandwagon based on convenience or our fear of rejection. That mentality doesn't benefit anyone. In actuality, it's that very cognitive bias by which we slip (not jump) from conviction to compromise, sacrificing our faith for the sake of conformity.

Paul encourages us not to fall into that trap but rather to do the opposite. He tells us that we need to be trendsetters. "Since then, we know what it is to fear the Lord, we try to persuade others … For Christ's love compels us, because we are convinced that one died for all … He has committed to us the message of reconciliation … We are therefore Christ's ambassadors" (2 Corinthians 5:11–21).

As believers, we aren't arguing our evidence and logic to convince someone to see things our way. We are a living demonstration of the equal opportunity for everyone to respond to the love of Christ. Our living testimony of being rescued and having a new life delivers the message of reconciliation—the truth that the old life is not only gone but also not counted against us. That hope and promise are what compel us, and they are what will convince them.

It's hard to live by faith and not by sight when we are busy comparing ourselves and our situations with everyone else's. But in God's grace, we are compelled to live life with a different focus. We no longer live with selfish intents. We realize that the old is gone and a new, better way has come, and we embrace it. We realize that our life—our new creation—has a new purpose to be His ambassador, His representation, in the world we live in.

When we continue through the first two verses of chapter 6, we see that now is the time of God's favor. Now is the time of salvation. It's not about what we don't have. It's not about COVID, the job we are trying to get, the war in Ukraine, or the future we can't yet see. It's about what God wants to do *in* and *through* you today amid your situation and your sphere of influence as His ambassador.

Have you fully left your old life behind? What are you still holding onto?

_____

_____

_____

_____

Although I firmly believe your life can be one of the greatest testimonies of proof to convince others to take a step toward Jesus, I also firmly believe we must also use our lips. "How, then, can they call on the one they have not yet believed in? And how can they believe in the one of whom they have not heard? And how can they hear without someone preaching to them?" (Romans 10:14).

This passage follows a very rational pattern and process. It all begins with you and me. We must do the "preaching" in word as well as in deed. "Preaching" in the Greek language means to "publicly announce gospel truth and principles while urging acceptance and compliance." This isn't just the job of your pastor. It's everyone's job to go into all the world and preach the gospel to everyone everywhere (Mark 16:15).

In our preaching, they can then hear of God's love and grace, believe in Him, and call on Him for salvation and new life, just as we have experienced. Our step of faith to tell (preach) gives them the opportunity here to take their own next step. "Consequently, faith comes from hearing the message, and the message is heard through the word about Christ" (Romans 10:17).

Make a list of those in your sphere of influence for whom God has positioned you to demonstrate His love and grace through word and deed.

_____

_____

_____

_____

Keep these names on your daily prayer list and ask God for wisdom and boldness to be His ambassador, as though God were making His appeal through you. Look for ways to put God on display in your life and make the most of opportunities to speak to others about the faith that made you new. "Devote yourselves to prayer, being watchful and thankful. And pray for us, too, that God may open a door for our message, so that we may proclaim the mystery of Christ, for which I am in chains. Pray that I may proclaim it clearly, as I should. Be wise in the way you act toward outsiders; make the most of every opportunity. Let your conversation be always full of grace, seasoned with salt, so that you may know how to answer everyone" (Colossians 4:2–6).

## Songs for Worship

"Awake My Soul" by Upper Room

**What Did You Read?**
1 Samuel 3:1–21, Recognizing the Voice of God

**What Did You Learn?**

_____

_____

_____

_____

_____

**How Can You Apply What You Have Learned to Your Daily Life?**

_____

_____

_____

_____

_____

**Prayer**

_____

_____

_____

_____

_____

## Songs for Worship

"First Love," "Embers," and "Obsession" by Kari Jobe

**What Did You Read?**
Ephesians 2:1–10, Alive in Christ

**What Did You Learn?**

_____

_____

_____

_____

_____

**How Can You Apply What You Have Learned to Your Daily Life?**

_____

_____

_____

_____

_____

**Prayer**

_____

_____

_____

_____

_____

## *Songs for Worship*

"You Really Are Beautiful" by Upper Room

**What Did You Read?**
Ephesians 2:11–22, The Church and Its Mission

**What Did You Learn?**

_____

_____

_____

_____

_____

_____

**How Can You Apply What You Have Learned to Your Daily Life?**

_____

_____

_____

_____

_____

**Prayer**

_____

_____

_____

_____

_____

_____

# *Songs for Worship*

"To Worship You I Live" by WorshipMob

**What Did You Read?**
Ephesians 3:14–21, Fill It to the Rim

**What Did You Learn?**

_____

_____

_____

_____

_____

**How Can You Apply What You Have Learned to Your Daily Life?**

_____

_____

_____

_____

_____

**Prayer**

_____

_____

_____

_____

_____

## *Songs for Worship*

"I Can't Get Away" and "Downpour" by Bethel Music

**What Did You Read?**
Ephesians 4:1–16, Working Together

**What Did You Learn?**

_____

_____

_____

_____

_____

_____

**How Can You Apply What You Have Learned to Your Daily Life?**

_____

_____

_____

_____

_____

**Prayer**

_____

_____

_____

_____

_____

_____

## Songs for Worship

"You Hold It All Together" by Maverick City and Upper Room

**What Did You Read?**
Ephesians 4:17–32, New Way to Think

**What Did You Learn?**

_____

_____

_____

_____

_____

**How Can You Apply What You Have Learned to Your Daily Life?**

_____

_____

_____

_____

_____

**Prayer**

_____

_____

_____

_____

_____

## Weekly Reflection _____

What were three *big* wins for the week?

1. _____
2. _____
3. _____

What were some of the game-changing lessons learned?

_____
_____
_____
_____

What are you grateful for this week?

_____
_____
_____
_____

How have you connected with others this week?

_____
_____
_____
_____

What has been your prayer focus and why?

_____
_____
_____
_____

## Notes and Ideas

## CHAPTER 12

# WHEN I AM AFRAID

When I was a kid, I was so afraid of the dark. I was convinced that there was something not of this world walking through my house in the middle of the night. I woke up and heard cracking from the house settling or a bump on the wall from another family member, and I froze in fear. Barely breathing, I listened for the next unexplainable noise, and my imagination ran wild.

Perhaps it was the scary stories my brothers shared. Maybe it was due to me watching too much sci-fi. It could've been the book I read by Lester Sumrall, in which he shared a story of casting out demons while on the mission field. Actually, it was most likely a combination of all those things. What I do know is that it followed me to my teen years, when I often left my closet light on so I could sleep.

Fear is real and at times an incapacitating emotion. We all face it, and we all learn to either live with it or overcome it. We can't just ignore it.

King David understood this, and he had a solution. He said in Psalm 56:3, "But when I am afraid, I will put my trust in you."

He didn't say, "*If* I am ever afraid, I will trust you." He very much expected it. He had experienced fear before, and he knew as a part of life that he would more than likely face it again.

I'm sure there was a healthy amount of fear in him when he faced the lion and the bear. What about Goliath? I would have been shaking in my sandals. Fear isn't all bad though, right?

Solomon had some wisdom about fear. He said the following:

> The fear of the Lord is the beginning of wisdom, and knowledge of the Holy One is understanding. (Proverbs 9:10)

> The fear of the Lord adds length to life, but the years of the wicked are cut short. (Proverbs 10:27)

> Whoever fears the Lord has a secure fortress, and for their children it will be a refuge. (Proverbs 14:26)

The fear Solomon was talking about means to honor, respect, revere, and be in awe. This respect and honor for God move us to live according to the boundaries in life He has established. Our reverence for God includes an understanding of His power and authority, and the consequences of stepping out of alignment with His character and commands.

Think about when people come into the presence of a king. They need to bow. Or when the judge walks into a courtroom, everyone needs to stand. Why? It's not fear like when I was a teenager in the dark—that irrational anxiety and unfounded intimidation. Instead, it's an expression of honor and an understanding that I need to respond to who is in the room. I need to demonstrate reverence because of their position; they are worthy.

So now what should I do with my fear? Fear of the dark; fear of failure; fear of being alone; fear of losing a relationship; fear of losing my job or not finding a job; fear of not being able to pay my bills; fear of my children making the wrong choices; fear of not being loved, accepted, or belonging?

Let me offer three insights:

1. *Shine a light on your fear.* As a kid lying in bed, afraid, I would muster the courage, jump out of bed, and turn the light on. I then realized the shadows, images, and noises— the things I perceived, the things I feared—weren't worthy of fear.

John 1:5 tells us that "the light shines in darkness, and the darkness has not overcome it."

Ask yourself, "What am I really afraid of?" What is the source of that fear? We know fear is not from God. In fact, fear is the antithesis of faith. God doesn't give us a spirit of timidity—a state of fear due to a lack of courage or moral strength; but He gives us power, love, and self-discipline. We can be confident in who is in the room with us and who He has made us to be.

2. *Arm yourself with God's truth.* Now that you've identified the source of your fear and know it's not from God and is actually the opposite of what God wants for you, arm yourself with scripture. The Bible is God's Word—God's breath of life—useful for teaching, rebuking, correcting, and training in righteousness. Use His Word to combat your fears.

If you fear being loved, accepted, or worthy, dig into scripture about how you are fearfully and wonderfully made, created on purpose with a purpose. You are God's masterpiece.

When you're afraid of a difficult circumstance or an important decision, find the scriptures that remind you that He is always with you. He is your God, He will strengthen and help you, and He will uphold you. You can be strong and courageous; His peace will guard your heart and mind.

Arm yourself with God's Word. When that fear reveals itself, speak those words over your life. Apply its truth. Pray those scriptures over that very fear you have identified.

In addition to arming yourself with God's Word, I would also encourage you to do battle in prayer and worship. Prayer and worship put God center stage in the midst of our fears. It will remove the attention away from fear and return it to its rightful place in God, from fear to faith. Get on iTunes, Spotify, Amazon Music, or YouTube. Make yourself a worship list. Put all your attention, honor, reverence, and respect on Jesus rather than on that fear.

3. *Don't face it alone.* Moses was afraid to speak to Pharaoh and the people, and God reminded him of his brother, Aaron, who could support him (Exodus 4:10–17). Esther had Mordecai when she was afraid to approach the king (Esther 4:14). Shadrach, Meshach, and Abednego had each other when they took their stand and faced the fiery furnace (Daniel 3:16–28).

Stop trying to face your fears alone. Share with someone what you are struggling with. Confess that fear. James tells us to confess our sins to each other and pray for each other so we can be healed. The prayer of a righteous person is powerful and effective (James 5:16). Where two or three are gathered together in His name, He is there, and it will be done (Matthew 20:18–20)!

Fear is a real struggle. We all deal with it. David, Joshua, Gideon, Ruth, Esther, and Mary faced it. When it happens, we don't give up. We don't lose hope. *When I am afraid, I will put my trust in God.*

We can overcome our fears. Shine a light on them. Arm yourself with God's Word and engage in warfare through prayer and worship. Don't face it alone. Let someone in on what you are growing through and let him or her walk with you through the process.

What are you afraid of? What is keeping you awake at night? What are the things you are not trusting God with?

_____

_____

_____

_____

_____

_____

Take some time and look up all the scriptures that speak to your fears. Then choose a few to memorize and have them ready for battle.

_____

_____

_____

_____

_____

Who are some godly friends and family you can share your fears with, knowing they will go to battle with you? Be intentional about talking with them and asking them to pray with you.

_____

_____

_____

The songs and scriptures for this week are very specific to this issue of overcoming our fears. Dig in deep and engage in warfare. The Bible app also has some incredible devotionals you can add to your routine.

## *Songs for Worship*

1. "No Fear" by Kari Jobe
2. "This Too Shall Pass" by Larry Fleet and Zach Williams

**What Did You Read?**

Psalm 23:1–6, The Good Shepherd

**What Did You Learn?**

_____

_____

_____

_____

_____

**How Can You Apply What You Have Learned to Your Daily Life?**

_____

_____

_____

_____

_____

**Prayer**

_____

_____

_____

_____

_____

## *Songs for Worship*

1. "Fear Is Not My Future" by Brandon Lake and Chandler Moore
2. "Ever Be" by Kalley and Bethel Music

**What Did You Read?**
John 14:15–27, The Promise of the Holy Spirit

**What Did You Learn?**

_____
_____
_____
_____
_____
_____

**How Can You Apply What You Have Learned to Your Daily Life?**

_____
_____
_____
_____
_____
_____

**Prayer**

_____
_____
_____
_____
_____

## Songs for Worship

"Most Beautiful / So in Love" by Chandler Moore

**What Did You Read?**
Deuteronomy 31:7–8, 23; Joshua 1:1–9; Fear Not

**What Did You Learn?**

_____

_____

_____

_____

_____

_____

**How Can You Apply What You Have Learned to Your Daily Life?**

_____

_____

_____

_____

_____

**Prayer**

_____

_____

_____

_____

_____

_____

## Songs for Worship

1. "Authority" by Elevation Worship
2. "Overcome" by Elevation Worship

**What Did You Read?**
Luke 12:4–12, Fear in Perspective

**What Did You Learn?**

_____
_____
_____
_____
_____
_____

**How Can You Apply What You Have Learned to Your Daily Life?**

_____
_____
_____
_____
_____
_____

**Prayer**

_____
_____
_____
_____
_____
_____

## *Songs for Worship*

"The One You Love" by Mav City and Kirk Franklin

**What Did You Read?**
Philippians 4:6–7; Proverbs 3:5–6; His Peace Is Our Strength

**What Did You Learn?**

_____
_____
_____
_____
_____
_____

**How Can You Apply What You Have Learned to Your Daily Life?**

_____
_____
_____
_____
_____
_____

**Prayer**

_____
_____
_____
_____
_____
_____

## Songs for Worship

"Too Good to Not Believe" by Brandon Lake and Cody Carnes

**What Did You Read?**
2 Timothy 1:6–14, Fear Is the Antithesis of Faith

**What Did You Learn?**

_____
_____
_____
_____
_____
_____

**How Can You Apply What You Have Learned to Your Daily Life?**

_____
_____
_____
_____
_____
_____

**Prayer**

_____
_____
_____
_____
_____
_____

## Weekly Reflection

What were three *big* wins for the week?

1. _____

2. _____

3. _____

What were some of the game-changing lessons learned?

_____

_____

_____

_____

What are you grateful for this week?

_____

_____

_____

_____

How have you connected with others this week?

_____

_____

_____

_____

What has been your prayer focus and why?

_____

_____

_____

_____

## Notes and Ideas

# CHAPTER 13

# LIVING IN COMMUNITY

During the summer between my junior and senior years of high school, I rode my bike over a thousand miles. My youth pastor, Ken Clark, got me into it, and I was training for a bike riding tour we were planning. The goal was to bike from Florida to Pennsylvania, stopping in various cities to do outreach and church services. The trip never did happen, but my passion for biking remained.

When I moved to Rhode Island for college, my bike came with me. There was a beautiful bike path that ran from Providence, near my school in Barrington, into Bristol. It took me past parks and golf courses, even to the beach. I didn't bike as much in college, but the scenery was great motivation.

After graduating from college, my wife and I took our first ministry position in Bushnell, Florida. I found another great bike path during my first week there. The terrain was so flat, and although it was early January, the weather was beautiful.

I mistakenly assumed that a twenty-five-mile ride would be a piece of cake. The fact that I hadn't ridden in several months didn't faze my young twenty-four-year-old mind. Worse yet, I thought one bottle of water would be enough to keep me hydrated.

About ten miles in, I ran out of water. I couldn't believe how much I was sweating in January. A few miles later, it dawned on me that I hadn't seen another adventurer like me for some time. First came the headache. Then my calves started to cramp. I was in trouble.

I dismounted my bike and just lay there on the side of the path, not sure what to do next. I didn't know how far the next crossroad was ahead of me, but I knew the last one I had passed was at least three miles back. I was alone and starting to worry (this was before the days of cell phones).

It may have only been ten minutes later, but it seemed like hours before I finally heard the tintinnabulation of a classic bicycle bell. I lifted my head to see an elderly man bringing his adult tricycle to a comfortable stop near where I lay on the grass. With a kind smile, he asked, "Did you run out of water?"

As he talked to me about how often he sees people stranded on this stretch of path, he handed me a water bottle and a bite-sized candy bar. What a lifesaver! I'm not sure what would have happened if he hadn't come along.

Unfortunately, many in life are in that very situation. They may not be physically dehydrated and alone on a bike path in the middle of Florida, but they are living isolated and empty on their journey of life. This was never God's intent for humanity.

The first problem in the world wasn't sin. It was solitude.

Go back to the story of creation in Genesis 1–2. God created man for relationships. He desired a relationship with Adam just as He does with you. A relationship is also the reason He created Eve for Adam. The account of creation records that all of creation was good until God noticed that Adam was alone.

Mankind was created in God's "likeness." He is a relational God; therefore, we are relational beings as well. We were created for God *and* for each other. Think of it as a communal gene—an embedded kind of DNA that is inborn, intentional, and inescapable.

Also, note that with it comes a distinct responsibility to be "fruitful and multiply" (Genesis 1:28). From the relational aspect, that means both vertically with God and horizontally with man.

Life wasn't meant to be lived in isolation but rather in community. *Community* literally means sharing common attitudes, interests, and goals. It's about having common unity. There is power in that unity and togetherness. Isolation, on the other hand, is lonely, empty, and destructive.

What Solomon shares in Ecclesiastes 4:9–12 is a clear indicator that we cannot be happily successful on our own. Not by a long shot. We will be helpless, lonely, cold, overwhelmed, and overpowered if we try to live life alone. *But* together in community, we can have a support system, a shoulder to cry on, someone to laugh and celebrate with, support in hard times, and the warmth and companionship for which we were created.

In community we carry each other's burdens (Galatians 6:2). We give each other the benefit of the doubt and forgive as we have been forgiven (Colossians 3:13–14). We demonstrate acceptance, humility, and unity (Romans 12:16; Galatians 3:28).

Look at what Paul says during the earliest stage of the formation of the church in Acts 2:42–47. They were onto something huge that would revolutionize their religious culture:

> They devoted themselves to the apostles, teaching and to the fellowship, to the breaking of bread and to prayer. Everyone was filled with awe at the many wonders and signs performed by the apostles. All the believers were together and had everything in common. They sold property and possessions to give to anyone who had need. Every day they continued to meet together in the temple courts. They broke bread in their homes and ate together with glad and sincere hearts, praising God and enjoying the favor of all the people. And the Lord added to their number daily those who were being saved.

This is the secret to community and evangelistic growth: "They continued together." They continued being the church when they left the church. They continued together doing relationally what they had experienced corporately. They grew larger by getting smaller. They became the church *in* the community and the hands and feet of Jesus *to* the community.

One of the most prolific discipleship experts, Dietrich Bonhoeffer, has been credited to have said, "The Gospel must be lived out not individually, but in community."[1] This follows well with one of my favorite scriptures from Hebrews 10:24–25: "And let us consider how we may spur one another on toward love and good deeds, not giving up meeting together, as some are in the habit of doing, but encouraging one another—and all the more as you see the Day approaching."

God will absolutely use His people—the church—to change the world. As our society becomes increasingly individualized, we can be tempted to practice our faith in isolation. But God created us for so much more. He intended for us to live in community.

What does community mean to you? What are some of the key words in your definition?

_____

_____

_____

According to your own definition, with whom are you currently living in community? How much time do you actually spend with them? What do you do together?

_____

_____

_____

Are you currently connected in a small group with other believers? If not, why not?

_____

_____

# Songs for Worship

"Getting Ready" by Maverick City and Upper Room

**What Did You Read?**
Act 2:42–47; 4:32–37; Living in Fellowship

**What Did You Learn?**

_____

_____

_____

_____

_____

**How Can You Apply What You Have Learned to Your Daily Life?**

_____

_____

_____

_____

_____

**Prayer**

_____

_____

_____

_____

_____

## Songs for Worship

"Lay It All Down" by Jesus Co and WorshipMob

**What Did You Read?**
Romans 12:1–21, Living Sacrifices

**What Did You Learn?**

_____
_____
_____
_____
_____
_____

**How Can You Apply What You Have Learned to Your Daily Life?**

_____
_____
_____
_____
_____

**Prayer**

_____
_____
_____
_____
_____
_____

## Songs for Worship

"Lion" by Elevation
"Reason to Praise" by Cory Asbury and Naomi Raine

**What Did You Read?**
1 Corinthians 12:1–31, You Belong

**What Did You Learn?**

_____

_____

_____

_____

_____

**How Can You Apply What You Have Learned to Your Daily Life?**

_____

_____

_____

_____

_____

_____

**Prayer**

_____

_____

_____

_____

_____

## *Songs for Worship* _____

"Make Us One" by Catch The Fire Music

**What Did You Read?**
1 Corinthians 13:1–13, Love Is Everything

**What Did You Learn?**

_____
_____
_____
_____
_____
_____

**How Can You Apply What You Have Learned to Your Daily Life?**

_____
_____
_____
_____
_____

**Prayer**

_____
_____
_____
_____
_____

## *Songs for Worship*

"I Will Exalt You" by Dante Bowe

**What Did You Read?**
Galatians 6:1–10, Doing Good

**What Did You Learn?**

_____

_____

_____

_____

_____

**How Can You Apply What You Have Learned to Your Daily Life?**

_____

_____

_____

_____

_____

**Prayer**

_____

_____

_____

_____

_____

## Songs for Worship

"Worthy of My Song" by Phil Wickham
"Where I'm Standing Now" by Phil Wickham

**What Did You Read?**
John 17:6–25, Jesus Prays for You

**What Did You Learn?**

_____
_____
_____
_____
_____
_____

**How Can You Apply What You Have Learned to Your Daily Life?**

_____
_____
_____
_____
_____
_____

**Prayer**

_____
_____
_____
_____
_____
_____

## *Weekly Reflection*

What were three *big* wins for the week?

1. _____
2. _____
3. _____

What were some of the game-changing lessons learned?

_____
_____
_____
_____

What are you grateful for this week?

_____
_____
_____
_____

How have you connected with others this week?

_____
_____
_____
_____

What has been your prayer focus and why?

_____
_____
_____
_____

## Notes and Ideas

CHAPTER 14

# HOW MANY TIMES?

I love road trips! I got this love from my dad. He would pile us into the car, and we would just drive. I was just a kid, and I don't remember much about the details, but I know I loved trips.

When I started driving, I continued the road trip tradition. One of my first ones was with my best friend, Mike, and we drove from Hazleton, Pennsylvania, to Trenton, New Jersey, to see the Newsboys and DC Talk in concert.

Before the days of GPS in cars and on phones, we had to rely on the *Rand McNally Road Atlas* and *AAA Trip Ticks*. They were these foldout maps, on which we had to highlight our route from point A to B. You basically needed a PhD in topography and a confident navigator. GPS was a game changer.

Sometimes you didn't need a map; you just followed someone who knew where he or she was going. "Just follow me," he or she said. How often did that work? The person never watched to make sure I was keeping up. He or she floored it when the light turned yellow and left me there at the red light. Or the person acted as if he or she were racing at Daytona, and my little Ford Escort could never keep up.

In Matthew 4, we find Jesus beginning His earthly ministry tour, and He was selecting His dream team. He handpicked guys to do life with and offered them an opportunity to be part of something bigger than themselves. One of the first guys he called was Simon Peter.

Peter was a fisherman by trade, and he was in his boat with his brother, Andrew. They were on the Sea of Galilee, casting their nets, minding their own business, and doing what they knew—running the family business. Jesus called to them and said, "Come follow me ... and I will make you fishers of men" (Matthew 4:19).

Their response is uncanny. "At once they left their nets and followed him." Both Luke and John's accounts shed a little more light on how the whole thing went down. Jesus had already been preaching and healing people, so they knew who He was and what He was asking of them. *Follow Me—be discipled by Me—together. Let's do some good. Let's make a difference and shake things up a bit.*

"Follow me" is almost like saying, "Come on a road trip with me."

Jesus wasn't looking for a companion; He was looking for a commitment from strangers. He was asking them to choose a whole new way of life—as if to say, "Follow Me. Join Me on this road trip of life. Career, family, status ... it all becomes secondary, an afterthought. Follow me. Forget the fish—we are going after something bigger."

Right there on the shores of the Sea of Galilee, Simon—called Peter—made a choice that altered the course of his life. He chose to follow Jesus.

This is the Simon Peter who later confessed that Jesus was the Christ, Son of the living God (Matthew 16:16). Jesus congratulated his answer with a name change of sorts." Blessed are you, Simon, because God revealed that to you, Peter, that revelation of truth will be the foundation of building His church" (16:17-18, my paraphrase).

This is the same Peter who, sixty seconds later, tried to correct Jesus about His coming suffering and death, and Jesus told him,

"Get behind me, Satan" (16:23). One minute: "Great answer!" The next: "Get behind me, Satan!"

This is the same Peter who, as he saw Jesus walking on water toward their boat in the middle of the night, said, "Lord, if it really is you, tell me to come to you on the water." Jesus said, "Come," and he stepped out of the boat and walked on water! Well, for a little bit, until he took his eyes off Jesus and saw the waves (Matthew 14:28–22).

This is the same Peter who was one of the three chosen to go with Jesus to the garden to pray but fell asleep when Jesus needed him most—twice (Matthew 26:36–46).

This is the Peter who, when they came to arrest Jesus, drew his sword and cut off the ear of the high priest's servant (John 18:10). Pretty bold!

Even though he declared, "Even if I have to die with you, I will never disown you" (Matthew 26:35), later that night, this same Peter denied Jesus three times (John 18:15–27).

It is Peter who, after seeing the empty tomb, still didn't understand that Jesus had to rise from the dead (John 20:9).

It's the same Peter who, after seeing the resurrected Christ, perhaps figured the road trip must be over and went back to fishing.

This is crazy because three-and-a-half years later, there Peter was, back on the same lake, back to doing the same thing he had been doing before Jesus called him to "follow me" (John 21:1–3). It doesn't necessarily mean he was giving up—he just didn't know what to do next.

So there they were, fishing all night, but they caught nothing.

Someone from the shore yelled to them, "Did you catch anything?"

They didn't realize it was Jesus yet, and they just yelled back, "No."

Jesus replied, "Throw your net on the other side of the boat, and you'll find some." And when they did that, they caught so many fish, they couldn't haul them all in.

Then it dawned on one of them that Jesus was the one yelling to them from shore. It was as if the proverbial light went on in their heads.

Perhaps Peter at that moment remembered that at that very spot three-and-a-half years before, the very same series of events had transpired (Luke 5:11; Matthew 4:18–20). So, in classic Peter form, he jumped out of the boat and swam to the shore to see Jesus, where they all ate some breakfast together.

> When they had finished eating, Jesus said to Simon Peter, "Simon son of John, do you love me more than these?"
>
> "Yes, Lord," he said, "you know that I love you."
>
> Jesus said, "Feed my lambs."
>
> Again Jesus said, "Simon son of John, do you love me?"
>
> He answered, "Yes, Lord, you know that I love you."
>
> Jesus said, "Take care of my sheep."
>
> The third time he said to him, "Simon son of John, do you love me?"
>
> Peter was hurt because Jesus asked him the third time, "Do you love me?" He said, "Lord, you know all things; you know that I love you."
>
> Jesus said, "Feed my sheep. Very truly I tell you, when you were younger you dressed yourself and went where you wanted; but when you are old you will stretch out your hands, and someone else will dress you and lead you where you do not want to go." Jesus said this to indicate the kind of death by which Peter would glorify God. Then he said to him, "Follow me!" (John 21:15–19)

I guess it's not surprising that Jesus asked Peter three times whether he truly loved Him. Peter would, after all, deny Him three times, right? I don't think it was so much a question of whether he loved Jesus but how much he loved Jesus.

I feel that "Follow me" includes three things: to become a disciple, to keep your eyes on Jesus, and to step into your calling.

1. Become a disciple. "Follow me" is a call to get out of the boat and make a personal commitment to be a disciple. It carries the weight of listening and learning. It means to join Jesus on the road trip of life and faith.

Notice I said to join Jesus and not to have Jesus join you. The invitation of salvation is for us to repent and walk away from our old lives to follow Him. He forgives. We follow. Following is more than a Sunday service experience. Following means we study God's Word for ourselves rather than waiting for a minister to spoon-feed us.

It also means we give people permission to speak into our lives. This best happens when we join a small group; experience deep, authentic connections; find freedom; and take next steps.

2. Keep your eyes on Jesus, not the waves. "Follow me" is a call to get out of the boat and walk on water. It's a test of our faith. The bigger, the better. Peter had to learn that, and so do we!

Keeping our eyes on Jesus requires that we pray. There is no sleeping on the job when it comes to faith. Trying to follow Jesus without a consistent prayer life is like running a car without oil. It will go for a little while, but eventually, you'll burn out the engine.

Keeping our eyes on Jesus also necessitates being filled with the Holy Spirit. In Acts 1:8, Jesus told the disciples to wait until they received the power and enablement of the Holy Spirit. Faith to do big things takes the power of the Holy Spirit. How much more do we need to wait and be filled?

3. Stand up, speak out, and step into your calling. "Follow me" is a call to step into your gift. Everyone has been given a special gift (Ephesians 4:7; 1 Peter 4:10).

Despite Peter's lack of speaking up when it would have counted on the night Jesus was betrayed, his gift was leadership and public speaking. Everything Peter had experienced up to this point, every "follow me" call he answered, led him to this very moment in Acts 2:14.

As the Holy Spirit was poured out and manifested through speaking in tongues, crowds curiously gathered around. Other Christians were amazed and confused. Others made fun of them and said they must be drunk.

This was Peter's moment. Empowered by the Spirit, he stood up, raised his voice, and addressed the crowd. His boldness and his voice were his gifts, and they were what God wanted all along. He was a leader, an influencer, and God wanted to use that to build His church. Everyone has a gift, and God wants to use it. He wants to use you to stand up, speak out, and address the crowd.

Maybe you're figuratively in the same boat as Peter. You had a momentous call to follow Him at salvation. You've walked with Jesus, and maybe at times it even seemed like you were walking on water. You've had some great spiritual encounters and experiences. You've gained knowledge of who He is, and your faith grew.

But then at times, you've doubted His power or purposes, maybe even to the point that you've compromised your convictions and denied Him by the choices you've made.

Perhaps after everything you've seen, heard, and experienced, you're confused about why God allows certain things. Your expectations haven't been met, and you just don't know what to do next. Like Peter, you've gone back to the same place you were before the whole road trip began. You're back to doing what's comfortable and easy. The result? Well, it's no different either—you're unfulfilled, unsatisfied, empty, hungry, and frustrated.

So how many times is it going to take? How many times does Jesus need to ask you, "Do you love Me?"

Everyone reading this, no matter where you are physically or spiritually, is being asked like Peter, "Do you love Me? Do you love Me more than a career, a relationship, your social status, your title, or the size of your bank account? Do you love Me?"

How many times will it take for Him to ask you to be His disciple and go all in? How many times will it take for Him to ask you to keep your eyes on Him, to walk by faith and not by sight? How many times will it take for Him to ask you to embrace what He's created you for and use the gifts He's empowered you with to make a difference in this world?

I don't know how many times Jesus has asked you. I can't tell you how many times He's asked me. What I do know, regardless of how many times it's been, is that He's asking you again today, "Do you love Me? Then follow Me."

"The Heart of Worship" by Upper Room

**What Did You Read?**
Matthew 10:1–16; Luke 9:1–6; Disciples Sent Out

**What Did You Learn?**

_____
_____
_____
_____
_____
_____

**How Can You Apply What You Have Learned to Your Daily Life?**

_____
_____
_____
_____
_____
_____

**Prayer**

_____
_____
_____
_____
_____
_____

## *Songs for Worship*

"Revelation Song" by Bethel

**What Did You Read?**
Matthew 10:17–42, Discipleship and Suffering

**What Did You Learn?**

_____
_____
_____
_____
_____
_____

**How Can You Apply What You Have Learned to Your Daily Life?**

_____
_____
_____
_____
_____
_____

**Prayer**

_____
_____
_____
_____
_____
_____

## Songs for Worship

"It Is So / There Is a Cloud" by Elevation Worship

**What Did You Read?**
Matthew 16:24–28; Mark 8:34; Luke 8:23–27; Take Up Your Cross

**What Did You Learn?**

_____
_____
_____
_____
_____
_____

**How Can You Apply What You Have Learned to Your Daily Life?**

_____
_____
_____
_____
_____

**Prayer**

_____
_____
_____
_____
_____
_____

# Songs for Worship

"Fountains / Came to My Rescue" by Bethel

**What Did You Read?**
Luke 14:25–35, The Cost of Discipleship

**What Did You Learn?**

_____

_____

_____

_____

_____

**How Can You Apply What You Have Learned to Your Daily Life?**

_____

_____

_____

_____

_____

**Prayer**

_____

_____

_____

_____

_____

_____

# Songs for Worship

"Holy Spirit I Surrender" by Chandler Moore

**What Did You Read?**
Colossians 4:1–18, Devote Yourself

**What Did You Learn?**

_____

_____

_____

_____

_____

_____

**How Can You Apply What You Have Learned to Your Daily Life?**

_____

_____

_____

_____

_____

_____

**Prayer**

_____

_____

_____

_____

_____

_____

## *Songs for Worship*

"Breathe" by Hillsong

**What Did You Read?**
Romans 12:9–21, Love in Action

**What Did You Learn?**

_____

_____

_____

_____

_____

**How Can You Apply What You Have Learned to Your Daily Life?**

_____

_____

_____

_____

_____

**Prayer**

_____

_____

_____

_____

_____

## *Weekly Reflection*

What were three *big* wins for the week?

1. _____
2. _____
3. _____


What were some of the game-changing lessons learned?

_____
_____
_____
_____


What are you grateful for this week?

_____
_____
_____
_____


How have you connected with others this week?

_____
_____
_____
_____


What has been your prayer focus and why?

_____
_____
_____
_____

# Notes and Ideas

## CHAPTER 15

# PRESS ON

I ran track and field during my junior year of high school. Before you get all excited for me, let me admit that it was a less-than-illustrious career. I competed in the eight-hundred-meter race, long jump, and the triple jump. I hate to admit it, but I never won. I never even placed. Sometimes even the girls finished before me.

I wanted to be the guy who stretched out and leaned forward just in time to cross the finish line first. I wanted to be the winner. I wanted to get the medal—any medal. Unfortunately, it never happened. I never got to celebrate at the finish line. My finish line experience was trying not to throw up in exhaustion.

Have you ever witnessed a close finish? It was the 2015 Pepsi Team Invitational, and an Oregon college student was competing in the steeplechase race with students from four other schools. With about fifty meters left to run, he had a decent lead and began to celebrate. He was waving his arms and trying to get the crowd to cheer for him and his school as he prepared to cross the finish line. Then in the last twenty-five meters or so, a runner from Washington sprinted past him and won the race by just a foot! I kind of felt bad for the Oregon student, yet I couldn't help but chuckle. The look on his face was priceless.

This story reminds me of 1 Corinthians 9:24. Paul says, "Do you not know that in a race all the runners run, but only one gets the prize? Run in such a way as to get the prize." That student thought he was running to win. He missed out on winning because he didn't run to win. He ran to celebrate, and that distraction cost him the victory.

This past week, I've been watching a little bit of the Track and Field World Championship. The competition for the Women's two-hundred-meter semifinal was fierce. The winner of this particular semifinal was determined by the runner's last effort to lean in! Her stretch and lean at the finish line was the one-one hundredths of a second difference between first and second place. It was an amazing photo finish!

For me, though, one of the best races of all time was from the 2016 Olympics in Rio. The women's four-by-four one-hundred-meter race became an epic story for the history books.

In the first round, Allyson Felix was about to hand the baton to her teammate, English Gardner, when a runner from the hosting Brazilian team bumped her. The baton fell fatally to the ground, and the American runners stood in awful disappointment. The crowd was stunned.

This story reminds me of Paul's remarks in Galatians 5:7: "You were running a good race. Who cut in on you to keep you from obeying the truth?" Allyson was literally cut off and kept from running.

Then Allyson composed herself, ran back to where the baton had fallen, picked it up, gave it to her teammate, and told her to run. *Finish the race, and let's figure it out later.* The world watched as the favored American sprinters ran the last two legs of the race, even though everyone had already finished.

Of course, the American team protested. The officials went back to the video and saw what had happened and granted them a new chance to run their race. The only catch was, they had to run it on an empty track. There would be no one to race against except the clock!

Now the pressure was on. All alone on the track with the world watching, they had to prove they could not only run without dropping the baton but also beat the time to get to the gold medal round. Well, run they did! Not only did they make the time needed to get to the next round, but they also recorded the best time of any team.

The next day, they returned to the track for the gold medal race. Suddenly, they faced yet another obstacle. It was the biggest race of English Gardner's life, and yet she had forgotten her shoes! There was no time to go back to the hotel and get them. They needed to figure something out quickly.

Luckily, Allyson Felix always had several pairs in her bag. The problem, however, was that they weren't the correct size. They were a half size too big. Have you ever walked with shoes that were too big on you? Try running in them, especially in a race with this much at stake. What choice did they have?

There was still one final piece of the mayhem they had to work through. Rather than being placed in the middle lane usually assigned to the team or person with the best qualifying time, the American team was assigned to lane one, which is usually assigned to the runner or team with the worst qualifying time. This is more of a mental issue than anything else, but ask any competitive runners, and they'll tell you; it makes a huge difference. Lane assignments matter.

Regardless of the circumstances—the wrong-size shoes, the unfortunate lane assignment—regardless of what had happened the day before, it was time to race. I loved the anticipation as they walked onto the track and got set in their blocks. Everyone's adrenaline was pumping. Everyone watching sat on the edge of his or her seat in silence.

The women's American team learned firsthand the application of James's words: "Blessed is the one who perseveres under trial ... [they] will receive the crown of life" (James 1:12). Those four women sprinters made history and won the race. They got the gold!

Let me share a final passage with you from Philippians 3:12–16. Paul is talking about how he wanted to know Christ and live confidently in a crazy world. He used an illustration his readers could identify with, one very similar to what I just shared about that Olympic team. "Not that I have already obtained all this, or have already arrived at my goal, but I press on to take hold of that for which Christ Jesus took hold of me. Brothers and sisters, I do not consider myself yet to have taken hold of it. *But* one thing I do: Forgetting what is behind and straining toward what is ahead, I press on toward the goal to win the prize for which God has called me heavenward in Christ Jesus" (Philippians 3:12–14, emphasis added).

Paul understood that he was never going to outgrow his need for grace. He was, like we all are, still working toward the goal. He was still pressing on. He actually said this twice. That indicates how important the point was that he was trying to make.

His words encourage us to forget our failures. Why would we hold onto them? God doesn't. The psalmist tells us that as far as the east is from the west, so far has God removed our transgressions from us (Psalm 103:12). God forgives, and He forgets. We need to focus on what lies ahead. We can't win gold by running backward. Keep our eye on the prize.

Paul continues in verse 15, saying, "All of us, then, who are mature should take such view of things. And if on some point you think differently, that too God will make clear to you." In other words, if you think differently, God will prove it to you.

Paul wanted for his readers the same thing he wanted for himself—to know God and to be persistent and consistent in his pursuit to win the prize. What is the prize? It's abundant life here on earth and eternal life in heaven when this life is over. It's the best life possible here and now and an even better life on the other side.

But if at some point you think differently or are unsure or doubtful—someone got in your lane and pushed you out—pick that baton back up and keep running. You forgot your shoes on race day? Take what's available and run. You're not in a favorable position to run, or your lane is not the lane you wanted? Keep your eyes on the prize and run to win.

Paul is encouraging us that God will give clear direction and He will make a way. James also challenges us that if we lack wisdom, if we lack understanding of our next steps, we simply need to ask for it. He will give freely without judgment or condemnation (James 1:5). Don't miss out on winning because you're too proud to ask Him for help.

Paul then closes his thought with this statement in verse 16: "Only let us live up to what we have already attained." He's telling us to live up to the grace God has already provided and the victory we have already achieved. No, we haven't arrived yet. We're not at the finish line yet. We're not yet on the podium, having that gold hardware placed around our neck. But for now, use this day as a mile marker. Press on!

Be grateful for where God has brought you by His grace, but don't yet be satisfied because He's not done yet. You're not done yet. Warren Wiersbe calls this a "sanctified dissatisfaction" (Wiersbe 1996, 88).

Spiritual maturity celebrates progress and victories while keeping the end in mind. We may be able to see the finish line, but we're not there yet. We may have been knocked off course at times, we may have dropped the baton, we may be wearing someone else's sneakers, or we may feel like we're not in the best lane, but it's race day. Yesterday is history, and tomorrow is a mystery, so today—right now—we press on.

## Songs for Worship

"When I Lock Eyes with You" by Upper Room

**What Did You Read?**
Hebrews 10:1–39, A Call to Persevere

**What Did You Learn?**

_____

_____

_____

_____

_____

**How Can You Apply What You Have Learned to Your Daily Life?**

_____

_____

_____

_____

_____

**Prayer**

_____

_____

_____

_____

_____

# Songs for Worship

"Endless Hallelujah" by WorshipMob

**What Did You Read?**
Hebrews 11:1–39, By Faith

**What Did You Learn?**

_____

_____

_____

_____

_____

_____

**How Can You Apply What You Have Learned to Your Daily Life?**

_____

_____

_____

_____

_____

**Prayer**

_____

_____

_____

_____

_____

_____

# Songs for Worship

"100 Million" by WorshipMob

**What Did You Read?**
Philippians 2:1–11, Imitating Christ

**What Did You Learn?**

_____

_____

_____

_____

_____

**How Can You Apply What You Have Learned to Your Daily Life?**

_____

_____

_____

_____

_____

**Prayer**

_____

_____

_____

_____

_____

# *Songs for Worship*

"The One You Love" by Chandler Moore and Elevation Worship
"I Love You Lord / I Exalt You" by Gateway Worship

## What Did You Read?
Philippians 3:1–11, Lose to Gain

## What Did You Learn?

_____
_____
_____
_____
_____
_____

## How Can You Apply What You Have Learned to Your Daily Life?

_____
_____
_____
_____
_____
_____

## Prayer

_____
_____
_____
_____
_____

*Songs for Worship* _____

"You Are Beautiful / I Want to See You" by Chandler Moore

**What Did You Read?**
Philippians 3:12–21; Hebrews 12:1–3; Press On

**What Did You Learn?**

_____
_____
_____
_____
_____
_____

**How Can You Apply What You Have Learned to Your Daily Life?**

_____
_____
_____
_____
_____
_____

**Prayer**

_____
_____
_____
_____
_____
_____

# *Songs for Worship*

"Have My Heart" by Maverick City Music

**What Did You Read?**
Philippians 4:10–20, Contentment

**What Did You Learn?**

_____

_____

_____

_____

_____

_____

**How Can You Apply What You Have Learned to Your Daily Life?**

_____

_____

_____

_____

_____

**Prayer**

_____

_____

_____

_____

_____

## Weekly Reflection _____

What were three *big* wins for the week?

1. _____
2. _____
3. _____

What were some of the game-changing lessons learned?

_____
_____
_____
_____

What are you grateful for this week?

_____
_____
_____
_____

How have you connected with others this week?

_____
_____
_____
_____

What has been your prayer focus and why?

_____
_____
_____
_____

## Notes and Ideas

## EPILOGUE

While I was growing up, my dad was a boxing fan. We often watched Friday-night fights together. One of his favorite fighters was George Foreman. As a nineteen-year-old high school dropout, Foreman won the gold medal in the 1968 Olympics in Mexico. He then became a professional fighter, winning forty straight professional fights, including a sequence of twenty-four consecutive knockouts. He went over five years without losing a fight until the infamous "Rumble in the Jungle," when he lost to Muhammad Ali.

His loss to Ali was devastating. He really didn't know how to lose. What many people don't know is that after that painful loss, Foreman tried desperately to get his reputation back. He actually set up an exhibition where he fought five guys back-to-back in one night, and he beat every single one! He was trying to force Ali into a rematch. He kept fighting and kept winning until he faced Jimmy Young and lost in the last round.

After that loss, Foreman hung up his gloves. He became a minister and founded the George Foreman Youth and Community Center in Houston. He was doing a lot of good for the kingdom. He was fighting the good fight, but he wanted to fight again in the ring.

Ten years after retirement, he returned to boxing. Once again, he took the sport by storm. Four years later, he had a chance to reclaim the heavyweight title, but he lost to Evander Holyfield. Two years later, he had another chance but lost to Tommy Morrison.

It was a great run. Why didn't he just retire again? Ali had retired a few years earlier with fifty-six wins, thirty-seven knockouts, and five losses. Foreman had fourteen more wins, thirty-one more knockouts, and one less loss. He had been fighting for over twenty years at that point; what more did he have to prove?

Foreman kept on fighting. At forty-five years of age and twenty years removed from losing the title to Ali, he got yet another chance to relinquish the throne. His opponent was the undefeated, 35–0, heavyweight champion of the world, Michael Moorer. Against all odds, Foreman knocked him out in the tenth round. Absolutely incredible!

How do you do that? How do you go from high school dropout to an Olympic gold medalist? How can you come back after ten years of being out of the game? How do you pick yourself up to fight again after such a devastating loss? How do you get over the age barrier and the criticism of fans and even colleagues? You do it by fighting another day. Foreman said, "I'm a winner each and every time I go into the ring." That was the key to his success. He got back in the ring.

As the apostle Paul was nearing the end of his life, he wrote a second letter to Timothy, whom he was mentoring. He said, "I have fought the good fight, I have finished the race, I have kept the faith" (2 Timothy 4:7).

Paul was a fighter. He fought against religious legalism and pagan idolatry. He fought against antinomianism and immorality in the church. He fought false teachers, the distortion of the gospel, worldliness, sin, and even his own thorn in the flesh.

Paul was also a finisher. There are two other times where the word *finished* is used in the Bible. The first is in Genesis; on the seventh day, God finished the work He had been doing in creation (Genesis 2:2). The next time is when Jesus was on the cross. After receiving a drink, He said, "It is finished." Then He bowed His head and died. Now in this verse, Paul told us he was finished. He wasn't quitting or giving up. There is a difference.

In 2 Corinthians 11:24–28, Paul gives us a list of some of the struggles he endured. He wasn't a quitter.

> Five times I received from the Jews the forty lashes minus one. Three times I was beaten with rods, once I was pelted with stones, three times I was shipwrecked, I spent a night and a day in the open sea, I have been constantly on the move. I have been in danger from rivers, in danger from bandits, in danger from my fellow Jews, in danger from Gentiles; in danger in the city, in danger in the country, in danger at sea; and in danger from false believers. I have labored and toiled and have often gone without sleep; I have known hunger and thirst and have often gone without food; I have been cold and naked. Besides everything else, I face daily the pressure of my concern for all the churches.

How many of us would have given up after just one of those things happened? Paul never gave up. When he wrote, "I have finished the race" to Timothy, he was in a Roman prison. Paul wanted Timothy to be a finisher as well. That's what I want, and I'm sure it's what you want as well.

I think the key to finishing the race is realizing that until I take my last breath, God isn't done with me. I love the words of the song "My Testimony" by Elevation Worship. "If I'm not dead, You're not done. / Greater things are still to come. / Oh, I believe."[1] If you're reading this, God isn't done with you yet.

### Don't quit.

Not only was Paul a fighter and finisher. He also kept the faith amid horrible circumstances. Nero was persecuting and killing Christians, and Paul was his prisoner in Rome, yet he kept the faith.

He suffered deprivation as a common criminal, but he kept the faith. Most of his friends deserted him; still he kept the faith. He was aware of his reality, that his ministry was over and death was near, but he kept the faith. "Now there is in store for me the crown of righteousness, which the Lord, the righteous judge, will award to me on that day—and not only to me, but also to all who have longed for his appearing" (2 Timothy 4:8).

Paul was able to keep the faith—keep believing, keep moving forward—because he was full of faith. He always trusted that God had a bigger picture in mind. He believed God was working all things for the good of those who love Him, who have been called according to His purpose (Romans 8:28).

You probably already know that one of the fiercest species of shark is the great white shark. Tons of movies have been made about this creature—*Jaws*, *The Shallows*, *The Meg*, to name a few. Great white sharks make the perfect villain with those menacing eyes and carnivorous teeth. Their acute sensitivity to smell blood in the water inherently triggers their survival instinct, and their hunger drives them.

A crazy fact you might not know is that if this particular species of shark stops moving forward, it actually suffocates and dies. It needs to keep oxygen-rich water flowing over its gills to stay alive.

I think that is a bit like our Christian faith. When we stop moving forward in our relationship with God, even just a little, we begin to suffocate our faith. Think of our faith as a fire. If we stop throwing logs on it, it burns out. We starve our faith when we stop moving forward. We stop moving forward because we stop believing.

Some people thought Paul was out of his mind (Acts 26:24–25; 2 Corinthians 5:13). The difficulties he endured, the persecution he suffered, the message he preached—they were all due to his insatiable desire to move forward in his faith. Paul was a fighter, a finisher, and he kept the faith because he knew his sweat and tears were watering the soil for tomorrow's victories. He was creating a legacy.

We need to fight for the things God cares about, things like our families, our communities, those without hope, and those who don't yet know Jesus, social injustice, righteousness, and the body of Christ.

We need to be finishers, not just starters. That means we follow up and follow through on our commitments. We don't give up when things become difficult. We persevere through suffering.

We need to keep the faith, keep believing, keep moving forward, keep growing, keep stepping out, keep being bold, and keep dreaming big.

Over the last twelve weeks, you have cultivated five spiritual habits. You have read scripture and learned how to meditate on it by searching for ways to apply its truth. You have taken time to pray and asked for God's hand to move on behalf of family, friends, and your community. You have journaled about the things you've learned and the prayers you have seen answered. You have practiced personal worship and developed a desire for that intimate time with God outside of the weekend church service. Finally, you have experienced the thrill of encouraging others by sharing with them what God has been teaching you.

I want you to know how proud I am of you. You have taken some great steps of faith and have grown in many ways. So, where do you go from here? What's next for you? May I offer a few suggestions?

Run to your favorite local bookstore and get yourself a good journal and a new pen. Stick with your pattern of daily time practicing The12. Make a new prayer list. Look up new worship songs from your favorite artists or church. Search the Bible app for some new devotionals or create your own reading plan. The point is, you have all this momentum. Celebrate but don't stop. Throw more logs on the fire.

Next, if you haven't already done so, get into a small group. It's more than just a cliché when we say we are better together. If you're not in a group, with whom will you pray? To whom will you confess?

Who will challenge your thinking and push you to go further? Iron can't sharpen iron if there's only one.

Finally, I challenge you to consider adding some spiritual habits to your repertoire. Discover the joys of generosity by giving your tithes and offerings to your church. Find a way to work fasting into your prayer time. Use your gifts and talents to serve your church regularly.

God has so much in store for you. He created you with big things in mind. Whether you have been walking out your faith for forty days or forty years, there is still more to learn, experience, and enjoy. Remember, you're not dead, so God's not done.

Keep fighting. Keep finishing. Keep the faith.

# NOTES

## Chapter One

1. Mark Batterson, *Win The Day* (Colorado Springs: Multnomah, 2020), 41.

## Chapter Three

1. "Sesame Street," Wikimedia Foundation, last modified January 12, 2023, 21:38, https://en.wikipedia.org/wiki/Sesame_Street.
2. The Pointer Sisters. "Pinball Number Count." Track 1 on *Sesame Street: Songs from the Street, Vol. 3.* Sesame Workshop Catalog, 2003, CD.
3. Bruce B. Barton, *Life Application Bible Commentary: John* (Wheaton, IL: Tyndale House, 1993), 86.
4. David Wheeler and Vernon Whaley, *The Great Commission to Worship* (Nashville, TN: B & H Publishing Group, 2011), 26-27.
5. Johannes P. Louw and Eugene A. Nida, *Greek-English Lexicon of the New Testament: Based on Semantic Domains*; electronic ed. of the 2nd edition, vol. 1 (New York: United Bible Societies, 1996), 141.
6. Warren W. Wiersbe, *The Bible Exposition Commentary*, vol. 2 (Wheaton, IL: Victor Books, 1996), 252.
7. James Swanson, *Dictionary of Biblical Languages with Semantic Domains: Greek New Testament*; electronic edition (Oak Harbor: Logos Research System, Inc, 1997).

8. Kenneth S. Wuest, *Wuest's Word Studies from the Greek New Testament: for the English Reader*, vol. 8 (Grand Rapids: Eerdmans, 1997), 150-151.

9. Ibid, 151.

10. Ibid.

11. Louw & Nida, *Greek-English Lexicon of the New Testament: Based on Semantic Domains*, 678.

## Chapter 4

1. Medium. "Life Is Like a Camera," accessed September 19, 2022, https://medium.com/@renewd_Life/life-is-like-a-camera-6aa34e7fdcd0.

## Chapter 5

1. Bruce B. Barton, Life *Application Bible: Philippians, Colossians, Philemon* (Wheaton, IL: Tyndale House Publishers, 1995), 160.

## Chapter 10

1. United Nations (@UN), "Fact: Nearly ½ of all fruit & vegetables produced globally are wasted each year: ow.ly/i/1p6Vt #ThinkEatSave #ZeroHunger," Twitter, January 26, 2013, 2:00 a.m., http://twitter.com/un/status/295078835282661377

## Chapter 13

1. Dietrich Bonhoeffer, *Letters and Papers From Prison* (New York: Touchstone, 1997), 123-124.

## Epilogue

1. Elevation Worship. "My Testimony." Track 1 on *Graves into Gardens*. Elevation Worship Records, 2020, CD.

# BIBLIOGRAPHY

Batterson, Mark. *Win The Day.* Colorado Springs: Multnomah, 2020.

Barton, Bruce B. *Life Application Bible Commentary: John.* Wheaton, IL: Tyndale House, 1993.

Barton, Bruce B. *Life Application Bible Commentary: Philippians, Colossians, Philemon.* Wheaton, IL: Tyndale House, 1993.

Bonhoeffer, Dietrich. *Letters and Papers From Prison.* New York: Touchstone, 1997.

Elevation Worship. 2020. "My Testimony." Track 1 on *Graves into Gardens.* Elevation Worship Records, compact disc.

Louw, Johannes P. and Eugene A. Nida, *Greek-English Lexicon of the New Testament: Based on Semantic Domains.* electronic ed. of the 2nd edition, vol. 1. New York: United Bible Societies, 1996.

Medium. "Life Is Like a Camera." Accessed September 19, 2022. https://medium.com/@renewd_Life/life-is-like-a-camera-6aa34e7fdcd0.

The Pointer Sisters. 2003. "Pinball Number Count." Track 1 on *Sesame Street: Songs from the Street, Vol. 3*. Sesame Workshop Catalog, compact disk.

Swanson, James. *Dictionary of Biblical Languages with Semantic Domains: Greek New Testament*. electronic ed. Oak Harbor: Logos Research System, Inc, 1997.

United Nations (@UN). 2013. "Fact: Nearly ½ of all fruit & vegetables produced globally are wasted each year: ow.ly/i/1p6Vt #ThinkEatSave #ZeroHunger," Twitter, January 26, 2013, 2:00 a.m. http://twitter.com/un/status/295078835282661377

Wheeler, David and V. Whaley. *The Great Commission to Worship*, Nashville, TN: B & H Publishing Group, 2011.

Wiersbe, Warren W. *The Bible Exposition Commentary*, vol. 2. Wheaton, IL: Victor Books, 1996.

Wikipedia. 2023. "Sesame Street," Wikimedia Foundation. Last modified January 12, 2023, 21:38. https://en.wikipedia.org/wiki/Sesame_Street.

Wuest, Kenneth. *Wuest's Word Studies from the Greek New Testament: for the English Reader*. vol. 8. Grand Rapids: Eerdmans, 1997.